# NGOs and Participatory Development in India

**About the Author**

**P.V. Baiju** holds Ph.D. in social work from Bharathidasan University Tiruchirappilli. He completed Master of Social Work from Rajgiri College of Social Sciences, Cochin in 1995 and subsequently Master degrees in Sociology and Economics and Bachelor in Law. He has worked in community development, water and sanitation, gender and development, HIV/AIDS, counselling, child labour and livelihood promotion. His expertise and research interests consist of participatory practices, gender and development, facilitation, holistic health, life skill and social work philosophy. He has completed externally aided five research projects in these fields. Baiju is a certified national trainer of Junior Chamber International, India, and conducts training sessions and facilitates workshops on multitude of topics to professionals and non-professionals. He is a consultant to many NGOs and government organizations in social development.

He contributed to development of social work profession in India by his active involvement in Indian Council of Social Welfare (ICSW), National Association of Professional Social Workers (NAPSWI) and Association of Schools of Social Work in Kerala (ASSK) and being member of International Association of Schools of Social Work (IASSW) and Asian and Pacific Association for Social Work Education (APASWE). Social work news (kerlamsw@googlegroups.com), that he founded is an active email group sharing information on social work conferences, scholarships and job openings in the country.

Baiju used to teach at Master of Social Work programme at Department of Social Work, Sree Sankaracharya University of Sanskrit. Kalady Kerala and is presently instructor at Faculty of Social Work, Red Deer College, Red Deer, Alberta, Canada.

# NGOs and Participatory Development in India

P.V. Baiju

CONCEPT PUBLISHING COMPANY PVT. LTD.
NEW DELHI-110059

**ISBN-13 : 978-93-5125-135-4**

First Published 2015

*Published and Printed by*

Concept Since 1974

**Concept Publishing Company Pvt. Ltd.**
A/15-16, Commercial Block, Mohan Garden
New Delhi-110059 (India)
*T*: 25351460, 25351794, *F*: 091-11-25357109
E: publishing@conceptpub.com, W: www.conceptpub.com
**Editorial Office: H-13, Bali Nagar, New Delhi-110 015, India.**

Cataloging in Publication Data—*Courtesy:* D.K. Agencies (P) Ltd. <docinfo@dkagencies.com>

**Baiju, P. V., author.**
NGOs and participatory development in India / P.V. Baiju.
pages ; cm
Includes bibliographical references (pages ) and index.
ISBN 9789351251354

1. Non-governmental organizations—India—Wayanad. 2. Non-governmental organizations—India. 3. Participatory rural appraisal—India—Wayanad. 4. Participatory rural appraisal—India. 5. Rural development—India—Wayanad. 6. Rural development--India. I. Title. II. Title: Non-governmental organisations and participatory development in India.

DDC 338.95483 23

# Preface

The development sector has unfolded numerous innovative models and strategies in the pursuit of creating a better world. The government and the non-governmental agencies have significantly contributed to such efforts. The initiatives of individuals and socially active groups too have given new hopes to the disadvantaged millions in the world. Interestingly the non-governmental agencies have been in the forefront of moulding new paths in the development arena, by virtue of their inherent advantages for experiments. Such attempts later are scaled up to macro spaces.

Of all concepts applied in human development, participation has become invariable as it aims at inclusive development of society. Participation assumes informed involvement of stakeholders in all realms of a programme that influences their life. It has received such an attention that all development process has incorporated elements of participation in them right from planning to evaluation of projects. Participatory Rural Appraisal, (PRA) has developed established forms of participation as well. The developing nations, including India, have significantly contributed to the development of participatory approaches. The NGOs in India and in Kerala have widely applied PRA in their projects as a method for stakeholder participation as well as for data generation.

This book is an attempt to understand the nuances of application of participatory approaches by the non-governmental organisations in Wayanad district of Kerala, India. The NGOs have applied participatory approach in various forms, especially through PRA. The donor agencies had made it mandatory to apply PRA at planning and implementation phases of many projects. However, many NGOs made use of PRA by its benefit in their programmes. The research explores the various factors of participation relying on the response of different stakeholders of NGOs. The research covers the profile of the beneficiaries of NGOs and the profile of the organisations. The study follows mixed methodology and analyses data from the view points of NGOs director, field staff and beneficiaries of NGOs programmes.

The book extensively covers NGOs sector in India with empirical data on NGOs and on.the profile of beneficiaries. The core theme of the book is participation and it carries wide discourse on it as well as on PRA and its field application. PRA had been the best participatory event and one of the best empowering processes for many NGOs. The beneficiaries too found it enjoyable, learning and growing opportunity. However, there had been challenges in field application of PRA. The findings of the research would be useful in devising more effective strategies for stakeholder participation in the development programmes by NGOs and government.

**P.V. Baiju**

# Acknowledgements

I am happy to publish this book and add to the literature on participatory development. Ever since my career as a social worker, I worked closely with NGOs. It has been a real wonder, the way NGOs work in this country, from the tiny single room office to corporate look like office, from meagre salaries to surplus corpus fund and fighting with government machinery to accessing all government sources. It was association with PLANET Kerala and M.J. Joseph that brought me closer to participatory practices and application of PRA in my work. A decade of being in NGOs sector and applying participatory methods led me to do my Ph.D. in the same topic.

I was fortunate to have a genius, empathetic and masterly guide for my research. I thank Dr. Selwyn Stanley, former Head of Department of Social Work at Bishop Heber College, Tiruchirappilli, for his wise guidance and patient mentoring. My gratitude is due to Dr. Umesh Samuel and Dr. P. Ilango, for their guidance and care as members of Doctoral Committee. Muhamamd Rafi, Jomet Jose and Rajesh K. extended their help in data collection at a time when I was not moving in my works and Dr. Sunanda helped me in tabulating the data. The six months fellowship from ICSSR helped me to relieve off my academic work and focus on my research. I appreciate and thank all of them.

It was the people in the NGOs in Wayanad, right from the Directors to field staff who spared their valuable time for me and shared knowledge, who helped in the field study of the research. The beneficiaries of NGOs, who found time for me and happily shared their experiences, were other significant contributors to this work. The personnel in the libraries I visited were kind enough to share the resources. My gratitude is to all of them as well as to those who shared their resources and encouraged me in this journey. My colleagues in different offices set a tone of support and encouragement by their wishful regards every time. And my students set me a high benchmark and this work is fulfilling their expectation of me, though not perfect in any sense. I thank Concept Publishing Co. Pvt. Ltd. for publishing this book and Shri A.K. Mittal for his support throughout.

Rincy, my wife, too joined for Ph.D. in the midst of my work. Professional interactions with her too enriched my research and she was pushing me to do it the best possible. It is a joy to live with our daughter Reese and son Ronn and an inspiration to make little achievements in life such as this. It was my parents who had absolute trust in me growing in education and rendered every penny for it and moments of prayer. It was not smooth sailing throughout this period of doing research and reworking to book. The Almighty had been always compassionate towards me in achieving simple success in life and celebrating this small life.

**P.V. Baiju**

# Contents

# List of Tables

# List of Figures and Exhibits

# Abbreviations

| | |
|---|---|
| BDS | Brhamgiri Development Society |
| CBO | Community Based Organisation |
| FGD | Focus Group Discussion |
| GoI | Government of India |
| GONGO | Government Organised Non-Governmental Organisation |
| JVALA | Joint Voluntary Action for Legal Alternative |
| NGO | Non-Governmental Organisation |
| NRM | Natural Resource Management |
| NWFDA | North Wayanad Forest Development Agency |
| PAME | Participatory Assessment, Monitoring and Evaluation |
| PME | Participatory Monitoring and Evaluation |
| PRA | Participatory Rural Appraisal |
| PLA | Participatory Learning and Action |
| PFM | Participatory Forest Management |
| PSH | Partnership in Sexual Health |
| PTD | Participatory Technology Development |
| RRA | Rapid Rural Appraisal |
| RASTA | Rural Agency for Social and Technological Advancement |
| SHG | Self-Help Group |
| ToT | Training of Trainers |
| VO | Voluntary Organisation |
| VOICE | Voluntary Organisation for Innovative and Collective Education |
| VSS | Vanam Samrakshana Samity (Forest Protection Committee) |
| WWA | Women Welfare Association |
| WSSS | Wayanad Social Service Society |

# 1
# Introduction

India boasts of a voluntary spirit in every realm of community life. The freedom movement in the country saw the pinnacle of voluntary movements and volunteers across the country worked hard not only for the freedom of the country but also for eradication of social evils and social development. After independence the Central and State governments launched series of programmes for community development. The voluntary spirit of the country was later integrated with scientific approaches and many organizations adapted to professionalism in community development. Government began to partner with Non-Governmental Organizations to reach to communities and deliver services. The role of NGOs in the country had been undisputable in the development of the nation, at its nook and corner. These organisations followed different innovative styles of implementing social development interventions and participatory practices were one of the important among them in the later part of twentieth century.

## Background of the Research

Kerala is considered as one of the most developed States in India. There are a multitude of factors that has led it to such an achievement, including social service agencies and social workers. The State has seen the changing faces of volunteerism, NGO intervention and professional social work in the post independent era. The voluntary work of people in the nook and corner of the

State in the form of local clubs, voluntary and charitable organisations, religious institutions, social activists and community leaders have contributed to the local level development of the State. These efforts have been hardly documented other than in the minds cf the people. Many such efforts continue in many parts of the State with modifications and variations in their nature and functioning. The voluntary organisations and activist movements based upon ideological themes also have been catalyst in influencing the people on radical ways as well as in charitable ways. The NGO activities that spread in the State in 1990s have deeply rooted in the society with the advancement of the sector supported by benevolent government policies.

The district of Wayanad is part of the Malabar region of Kerala. This district is considered one of the most backward in the region. The inhabitants of the district consist mostly of the tribal communities and migrant farmers. It is rich in natural resources with rivers and large area of forest, including the Muthanga National Park. The main occupation of the people is agriculture. The suicides of farmers due to the crisis in agriculture had attained national attention in 2006 and 2007. The people belong to Christians, Hindus, Muslims and small percentage of Jains. The district borders with the southern States of Karnataka and Tamil Nadu. The climate change has adversely affected the agriculture fortune of the farmers and planters, while tourism has started to flourish thanks to lush greenery and waterfalls. It is famous for the pilgrim centres and historical monuments.

Owing to its backwardness the district has witnessed the emergence of activists, the highest performance of Naxalite (radical Marxist activists adopting violence for social change) movement in the State and the intervention of the NGOs. Most of the actions of the Naxalite movement that shackled the social psyche of the State in 1970s happened in Wayanad. The district has more than one hundred active NGOs working among different groups in different locations and with varying ideology. The presence of large percentage of tribal has attracted NGOs in the area. The NGOs operate in different fields like agriculture, women development, rural development, tribal development, water and sanitation, natural resource management, rehabilitation and support services, counselling and science and technology. The

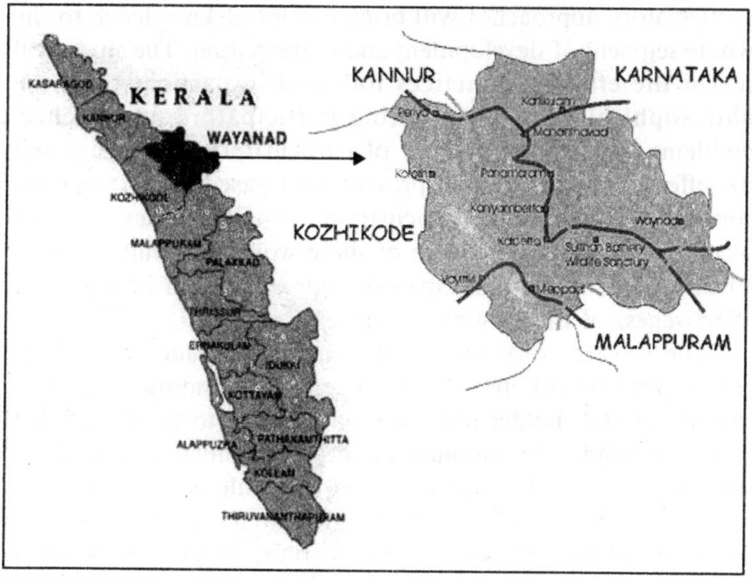


**Exhibit 1:** Wayanad District, Kerala

NGOs in Wayanad has widely followed participatory approaches in development and some of them pioneered the use of certain PRA tools. Few of them provide training on participatory approaches in development as well. Their impact has been significant to this district, as they have produced radical changes in the thinking of people, led to emergence of leadership, promotion of peoples' groups and advancement in the life of people. The district of Wayanad stands apart in the number of NGOs and in their intervention. Hence, the researcher has selected Wayanad for the study.

## Significance of the Study

The ever growing experiments in development lead to more effective use of resources and efficient systems for managing them. While participation is the key word in development, it is the NGOs who pioneered the participatory approaches in the development process. The spirit of participation had brought forth qualitative changes in the lives of people as well. A study about the participatory approaches will bring out lot of knowledge to the whole segment of development and participation. The study will reveal the effective practices followed in participation, the philosophical basis of adopting participatory approaches, problems faced in the practice of participatory approaches and the effect of them. It shall present field based information on concept and practice of participation by NGOs in development sector. The knowledge source of these would hopefully, help in advancement of the participatory approaches and improve the effectiveness of the existing systems.

The research outcomes shall benefit the academicians and practitioners at different levels. The understanding from field realities of stakeholder participation will add to the knowledge source of academic community. The development practitioners shall get first hand information on the philosophical basis of participatory approaches, methods followed and the problems faced form the actual experience of certain NGOs. The findings of the study shall aid for scaling up participatory approaches in the non-governmental sector. It shall also contribute to critical awareness on the practice of participatory approaches followed by the NGOs.

The study is expected to produce valid literature in the context of NGOs, their beneficiaries and participation and NGOs. The NGO sector is gaining momentum in the whole nation and their significant growing. Hence, a study on the characteristics of NGOs and the profile of their beneficiaries can enlighten on their status. The development sector would be added with new knowledge generated on the concepts and application of participatory approaches, NGOs intervention to promote stakeholder participation, the issues faced in stakeholder participation and the significance of established participatory approaches like PRA.

The study is particularly relevant in Malabar region of Kerala where the intervention of NGOs is very relevant and indeed essential. The development players have found participation as an important constituent in the whole development process. The study shall brighten the factual information on participation and its manifold features. The government sector, particularly in Kerala has increasingly adapted to participatory approaches. The State agencies also can find adaptable learning from the study.

The researcher hopes that this study will open new vistas for further research. The broad areas could be role of NGOs, concept of participation, tools for participatory approaches and level of participation by different stakeholders. The literature from this study also shall enrich the existing writings on participation and development.

**Statement of the Problem**

Participation has acclaimed an established recognition and application in the development process at the Government and Non-Government sectors. The emergence of Participatory Rural Appraisal (PRA) preceded by Rapid Rural Appraisal (RRA) and followed by Participatory Action and Learning (PLA) promoted by Robert Chambers (Mukherjee, 1997), has given a new dimension to participatory approaches. The idea of participatory approaches were carried out into almost all the parts of the world especially in the third world countries by the experts in PRA and by NGOs.

As a result of this paradigm shift from centralized planning and implementation to decentralized discussion and decision-making and participatory action, lot of participatory intervention models have been developed. Apart from PRA and PLA, PME (Participatory Monitoring and Evaluation), PTD (Participatory Technology Development), PFM (Participatory Forest Management), etc. have come up. There is enormous people's participation in the development initiatives, leading to effective output and impact through application of participatory tools. The world acclaimed Peoples Plan Campaign in Kerala is an example of how participation has been absorbed to democracy as well.

The true spirit of participation lies in accepting the last considered individual, group and institutions and giving them due share in decision-making or putting the last first (Chambers, 1997).

A change in the attitude of development practices is essential for such a change. The NGOs have been widely using participatory approaches in development by their own vision of development and by the force of partner agencies. The participatory approaches in the end have witnessed series of changes and institutionalization. The research focuses upon the participatory approaches followed by the NGOs.

Adaptation of participatory approaches requires changes in the policy of the organisation and attitude in the personnel of the agency. The concept of participation tries to include all the stakeholders of a project at different levels of a programme. It includes programme planning, implementation, monitoring and evaluation. The people friendly tools of PRA are effective in needs assessment and prioritisation of problems. The PME methods help for participatory monitoring and evaluation of a project. The tools in PRA are just the means to express the participation. The attitude for an inclusive approach and behaviour of the stakeholders is more important than tools.

A development programme is owned and benefited by the partners especially by the end receivers of its benefits. But traditionally the projects were designed and implemented by the project holders (NGOs and Government agencies) for the other partners. Participatory approaches have brought forth significant changes in this practice by giving ownership of a programme to its partners. The participatory development offers space for the illiterate, inefficient and downtrodden to raise their voice in the development initiatives.

The word participation has become a much used word in development so that its true meaning and application is faded or unclear. In the case of NGOs the donor organization has made it a mandate to do participatory assessment of the target groups for the project approval. Hence, participation has just been done even without genuine interest and unjust to its meanings. It has become imperative to uncover the meaning of participation as practiced by NGOs, the strategies followed by them for application of participatory concepts, the problems they face and impacts.

The Non-Government sector has embarked upon significant changes in the social development of the district. A study on participatory approaches of NGOs necessarily needs to include the NGOs and their target groups. The analysis seeks to understand the profile of the NGOs in their activities, staff pattern, networking, financial affairs and resources. On the profile of the beneficiaries an analysis would cover their socio-demographic profile, association with NGOs activities and decision-making process of their community based organisations.

The study would answer in detail various questions in this context. They include the profile of the NGOs in the district and the profile of the beneficiaries of the NGOs. What are the means employed by them to attain participation? What is the level and type of capacity development for the personnel in the organization for participation? What is the significance and reliability of participatory approaches followed by NGOs? How are PRA methods used by them? What are the effects of adopting participatory approaches? How do the stakeholders view the participatory approaches followed by the NGOs? What innovations have the organizations done to ensure participation? What problems and difficulties the organisations face in resorting to participatory methods? These questions call for an empirical study. This study is a search to a fuller understanding of participation as practiced by NGOs. The general aim of this research is, therefore, to study the participatory approaches for development followed by the NGOs in Wayanad District. The research questions formally addressed in this study are the following:

**Research Questions**

1. What are the characteristics of NGOs implementing participatory approaches?
2. What is the profile of the beneficiaries involved in participatory programmes?
3. Where all the NGOs apply participatory methodologies?
4. What are the various training activities done by the NGOs to promote stakeholder participation?
5. How is the involvement of the various stakeholders in the participatory process?
6. Which PRA tools do the NGOs apply for various purposes?

7. What are the advantages of using participatory approaches?
8. What are the problems faced by the NGOs in adopting participatory approaches?
9. What learning the NGOs could contribute for appropriate participatory methods in development programmes?

**Scope of the Study**

The research on the participatory approaches of NGOs covers the growing sector of participatory approaches by NGOs in development practice. The study unearths the profile of the NGOs in district. It will enable in the study of the non-government sector in the social development sector of the district. Similarity, the study would give a detailed account of the beneficiaries of the NGOs which shall facilitate for a deeper understanding of the target groups of the NGOs.

The Non-Governmental Organisations apply various tools developed in different parts of the world in ensuring the participation of the stakeholders and the people in general. The philosophy of the participatory approaches is important than the tools. The scope of the study is wide opened to the philosophy, tools and practices of the PRA in the field by the NGOs. The scope of the study is extended to the concept, approaches, techniques and mechanisms for participation. It would also examine the application of participation in the perception of beneficiary groups as well. Certain related areas like the network with other player in the development sector have not been included in the study. The study has not taken into account the participatory approach in the governmental and Panchayati Raj Institutions (PRIs) which are closely related in the development of the region.

The geographical area of the study is limited to Wayanad. The scope of the study in this context is that the study is done in the district that has the highest number of active NGOs in the State and they have touched all sectors of development as well as considerable population of the district. Even though the study is limited to only one district in the State the finding of the study could be generalized to other parts of the State as well as they represent a cross-section of the NGOs in the State as well as policies and practices of the NGO community in the State.

The scope of the study is also opened to the organizational and activity realms of the NGOs. The study interacts with the heads, staff and beneficiaries of the organisations, which shall bring data on the NGO sector in the State. The research would cover the administrative pattern of NGOs, the areas of activities, the infrastructure facilities, the details of staff and the target population. This can give a profile view of NGOs in Kerala. The scope of the study is opened to NGO sector, Participatory approaches in Wayanad. The study is limited to Wayanad district of Kerala and only to the participatory approaches of the NGOs.

## Conceptual Definitions

### *Participatory Approaches*

'Participatory approaches seek to understand human experiences as is and felt by the participants, the context of such experiences in an interdisciplinary framework.' (Mukherji, 2002)

### *NGOs (Non-Governmental Organisations)*

A voluntary organisation (used synonymous to NGO in this study) is a social service and developmental institution motivated to meet the needs of the most disadvantaged in society, either through direct services the people or through facilitative/indirect services to other voluntary organisation on government; non-profit making and not undertaken to be fully funded for its maintenance, directly of indirectly by the government. (Rana, 2001)

## Operational Definitions

### *Participatory Approaches*

Participatory approaches, in the present study means adapting to participatory methodologies of Participatory Rural Appraisal and its various forms in the programme planning of the organisations, where all associated parties (stakeholders) in a particular programme or project meant for the development of the parties, take part in the planning, implementation, evaluation and follow up of such programmes in such a way that they contribute and take benefit from the programme.

### *NGOs (Non-Governmental Organisations)*

Non-Governmental Organisations are those statutorily registered organisations working for the development of people in specific region or sector, in unison with local people appointing voluntary and/or paid staff and mobilizing resources from different government approved sources.

### *Wayanad*

Wayanad in this study means the revenue district of Wayanad in Kerala.

## Research Design

The study follows the mixed methodology of quantitative and qualitative research methodologies. With the development and perceived legitimacy of both qualitative and quantitative research in the social and human sciences, mixed methods research, employing the data collection associated with both forms of data, is expanding (Creswell, 2003). Combining methods, or employing triangulation, in a single research project is increasingly advocated on that it helps to facilitate a more valid and holistic picture of society that which could be acquired by remaining true to only one set of methods.

Many social researchers use 'multiple strategies of field research in order to overcome the problems that stem from studies relying upon a single theory, single method, single set of data and single investigator' (Burgess, 1984). According to Henn *et al.*, (2006), this approach is frequently referred to as triangulation. It suggests that research conclusions that are derived from converging evidences — using a variety of different research methods are likely to be more credible than research findings, which are based only on one source. Henn narrates on the advantages of combined methods. Methods are combined not only to gain their individual strengths, but also to compensate for the particular faults and limitations of any single system. Another reason for combining approaches using triangulation is to overcome bias in research. The third key advantage for adopting a multi-strategy approach in the research is that it is likely to assist in gaining a complete overview of the matter under investigation. The multi-strategy research approach, therefore, enables (and encourages) the researcher to investigate a particular research area from a variety of different angles and perspectives, focusing on different question and issues, collecting different types of data, analysing his data using different techniques, and interpreting the results from a variety of different positions.

Among the various methods in mixed methods (called as multiple methods as well) the study follows concurrent triangulation strategy. Concurrent triangulation model is selected when a researcher uses two different methods in an attempt to confirm, cross validate or corroborate findings within a single study (Greene *et al.*, 1989). This model generally uses separate quantitative and qualitative methods as a means to offset the weakness inherent within one method with the strength inherent in other methods. The quantitative and qualitative data collection is concurrent, happening in one phase of the research study. This strategy usually integrates the results of the two methods during the interpretation phase. This approach can result in well validated and substantiated findings. At the same time it requires great effort and expertise to adequately study a phenomenon with two separate methods (Creswell, 2003). Having done that the researcher has to manage the task of comparing the data of different forms and resolve the discrepancies of that may arise in the results. In this study the researcher hopes to manage it well as the findings of the study are very specific phenomenon.

The study had two important streams of data, namely the NGO and the people. The head and the staff represent the NGO, while the beneficiaries of the NGO constitute the people. The research questions were asked to them. The following exhibit shows the conceptual map explaining the streams of data, the important variables and the methods of data collection.

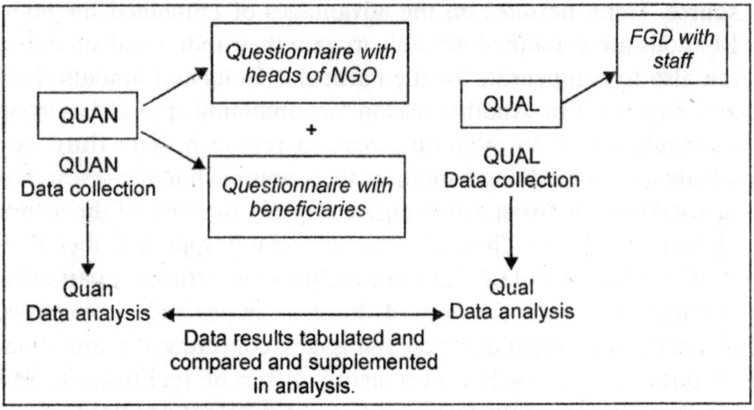


(Based on Creswell, 2003, 214).

**Exhibit 2:** Concurrent Triangulation Strategy in the study

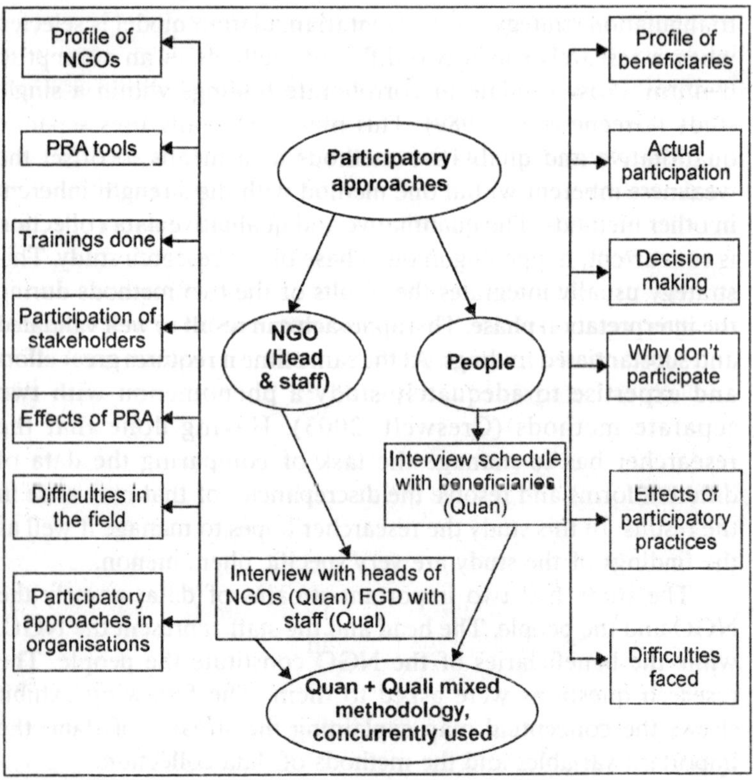


**Exhibit 3:** Conceptual Diagram explaining Streams of Data

The two major streams of the source of data are the NGO and the beneficiaries. The NGO consisted of the heads of the organisation and the staff while the people consist of the partners or beneficiaries of the organisation who has been part of the participatory programmes in the field. The parallel columns linked by arrows indicate the variables of study. The variables emanate from the research questions.

### *Pilot Study*

The researcher had first hand experience of the region and some NGOs there as part of the academic involvement. The researcher has undergone training in participatory approaches, which also has helped in formation of the preliminary concept of the study. The researcher has personally visited four NGOs, more than once, in the district in a span of four years. A detailed discussion with the heads of the organisation, the staff and the beneficiaries of the RASTA in August 2006 also helped to gain more insights on the practical aspects of data collection.

The initial approach for the study was done by consulting the practitioners of participatory approaches in the State, especially those among the members of Participatory Learning and Action Network, Kerala. (PLANET Kerala, Thiruvananthapuram). The researcher held discussions chief functionaries of Wayanad Social Services Society (WSSS), SHREYAS and RASTA. The feasibility of the study was ascertained by the discussions with them. It also clarified the concepts of the study.

### *Universe of the Study*

The universe of the study consisted of all the NGOs adopting participatory approaches in their community level programmes in Wayanad district. The inclusion criterion for selecting the NGOs for the study were the following:

- Legally registered and active with programmes for at least last three years.
- Active presence in at least two Grama Panchayats.
- Staff strength of not less than 10 (including voluntary staff).
- Annual turn over of Rs. two lakh and above.
- Seriously taken up participatory approaches in development for at least three years.

The NGOS selected on the above criteria were the following:

1. Arsha Bharath, Meppadi;
2. Brahmagiri Development Society (BDS), Meenanagadi;
3. Joint Voluntary Action for Legal Alternative (JVALA), Kalpetta;
4. Rural Agency for Social and Technological Advancement (RASTA), Kambalackad;
5. Shreyas, Sulthan Battery;
6. Voluntary Organisation for Innovative and Collective Education (VOICE), Sulthan Battery;
7. Wayanad Social Service Society (WSSS), Mananthavady;
8. Women Welfare Association (WWA), Vaduvamchal; and
9. North Wayanad Forest Development Agency (NWFDA), Mananthavady.

The NWFDA is initiated by the Forest Department, Government of Kerala. It has a legal entity of an NGO and works in the local community, but is largely managed by the government. This is included to compare the effect of PRA in the government initiated organisation. Two other organisations namely Area Development Programme, World Vision, Kalpetta, and High Land Area Development Association (HILDA) Sultan Battery have had application of PRA programmes, which the researcher contacted to include in the study. The HILDA has largely withdrawn from their field programmes and did not have personnel to attend to the research. The World Vision declined to participate stating they were busy with their internal evaluation at the time of data collection.

***Primary Sources of Data***

All the NGOs in the universe comprised the sample of the study. The respondents consisted of three categories:

1. The Heads of organizations represented either by the Director or Project Manager, next to the Director. Questionnaire was applied to them;
2. The staff of the NGO, who had been involved in the practice of participatory practices. An FGD in every NGO with five to eight staff; and
3. The beneficiaries who had been part of any participatory approaches of the organization in last ten years. Ten beneficiaries, representing at least two different CBOs, from one NGO were selected on random basis. Interview schedule was applied to total eighty beneficiaries.

**Secondary Sources of Data**

1. Registration certificate of the organisation;
2. Published reports;
3. Audited statement of accounts;
4. Evaluation study of organizations;
5. Press reports; and
6. Consultative meeting with the heads of the organization.

***Tools of Data Collection***

As the study followed a mix of quantitative and qualitative approaches, the methods of data collection in both methods are used in the study. The respondent category included the heads of the organisation, staff of the organisation and beneficiaries. The beneficiaries were those who have participated in a programme of participatory approach in the field and availed the benefit of the programme. They were mostly the leaders of the CBOs promoted by the NGO. The following instruments were used in the study.

1. ***Interview schedule with heads of the organisation:*** This was

applied to the organisation to collect the data of NGOs. The questionnaire had questions on the general profile of the organisation, areas of intervention, trainings done on participatory approaches, how they view participation and problems and effects of participatory approaches.

2. *Focus Group Discussion (FGD):* It was applied with the staff of the NGO. FGD was used with five to eight staffs of the organisation that have had experience in the participatory approaches of the organisation. This brought out data on their concept of participation and experiences in the field. As the field experience of application of participatory approaches was not that empirical qualitative forms of data collection was ideal. FGD was conducted with the staff in all the nine NGOs under study.
3. *Interview schedule with beneficiaries.* The beneficiaries of the programmes of the NGOs participate in the participatory programmes of the NGO and bear vision on the activities of the NGOs. The interview schedule carried questions related to the objectives of the study. The interview schedule was applied to ten beneficiaries representing at least two CBOs in the NGOs under study. The total respondents were ninety.

**Pretest**

The researcher applied the questionnaire for the heads of the organisation at Women's Welfare Association Vaduvamchal in the third week of December 2007. The researcher held the FGD with staff of WWA in May 2008. The interview schedule for the beneficiaries was tested among the beneficiaries of the VOICE and SHREYAS in the third week of May 2008. Certain questions with regard to tools of PRA in the questionnaire for the heads of NGO and the interview schedule were modified after the pretest. The questions on the profile of NGOs were sharpened after the pretest. The application of the tools of the study brought out feasibility of the study and enlightened on the areas to be added.

The pretest contributed to the skills required for data collection of the study.

**Data Collection**

The researcher collected the quantitative and qualitative data simultaneously. The period of data collection was from July to December 2008. The data collection was an interesting experience with slight difficulty. The difficulty was in scheduling the field visit to meet beneficiaries and to arrange FGD with staff. The beneficiaries could not get the names of the PRA tools where the researcher explained them in terms of how it looks like or they were done; for example, drawing the map on ground or putting *chapati* shaped circles, etc. It was difficult to reach the beneficiaries at remote areas. There was an incident in BDS where one beneficiary respondent waited for two hours as the researcher found it difficult to get a vehicle to reach him from another distant location. It was difficult to get the field staff involved in PRA together for FGD as they had busy field schedules. Moreover, as PRA was actively implemented in many NGOs five to ten years back, those who practiced had moved out of NGO. Hence, the researcher got three to six participants in the FGD as against proposed five to eight staff.

But reaching the beneficiaries and the staff on the field experiences of participation was exciting. All the beneficiaries who had attended the PRA workshop (some of them three to ten years back), had detailed memory of the activities took place in the workshop as well as on the effect of it. Moreover, many of them were eager to share their experiences, along with smiles in their face. But the most elating part of the data collection process was the FGD with staff. They shared their experience of conducting PRA in various locations as best field experiences of their NGO career. Every staff had his/her unique incident in the field to share with. Moreover, almost all groups recollected at least one story that changed the community as a result of PRA workshop in the target area. The staff voluntarily displayed the documented sheets of the PRA and the PRA reports, still kept in the offices, to the researcher. The data collection with the heads of the NGO was done with prior appointments. The directors (the chief executive officer) of five NGOs directly answered the questionnaire, while the project manager next to the director did it in four organizations.

## Data Analyses

The analysis of data followed the mixed methodology in research. According to Henn *et al.*, (2006), the analysis of data in mixed method, while focusing on the research questions, has a dual purpose of aiding research design and refinement. Analysis of data does not represent a final stage in the research process, but a stepping stone between stages. Another common reason for combining methods is that of data triangulation. The idea of triangulation stems from the geographical term whereby if the distances between two known points and at third point are taken, the exact position of the third point can be located. While in triangulation, both methods remain focused on the same point, which in this case is the research question.

According to Cresswell (2003), data analysis in mixed method occurs both within the quantitative and the qualitative approach, and often between the two approaches. As the Exhibit No. 2 explains the findings of both methods were simultaneously analysed. The analysis was based on each objective and related variables of the study. The multiple methods helped in triangulating and corroborating data. The quantitative data required application of statistical methods in the presentation and analysis. The qualitative data was scientifically analyzed and interpreted. The data was concurrently documented and analysed. The profile of the NGOs and beneficiaries are presented with simple tables and figures. The data on participatory approaches are triangulated and presented with tables and figures.

## Limitations of the Study

The study is limited by different methodological and environmental factors. The concurrent collection of quantitative and qualitative data collection paused challenges to the researcher in the logistic arrangement of the matters. The researcher managed them by effective planning for data collection. The researcher is fresh in application of mixed research methodology in research which the researcher attempted to overcome through references and discussions with experts. The NGOs in Kerala vigorously followed participatory approaches in late ninety-nineties. As the study is done in a period that is not at the peak of performance of practice of PRA the respondents found difficulty in answering certain questions. Similarly, the frequent change of staff of NGOs affected the availability of staff involved in participatory practices. The beneficiary respondents of the study mainly belonged to the CBOs where watershed project are implemented by the NGOs for PRA was recently done in watershed projects. This might have limited the perception of the beneficiaries from other segments in formulating the opinion on the NGOs.

# 2

# Non-Governmental Organizations in Development

## Introduction

The Non-Governmental Organizations have unequivocally claimed a significant place in the development sector. There is an enhancing space open for third sector (the voluntary sector, as the first sector (the government) increasingly withdraws from social welfare measures and the second sector (corporate) exists for profit. The NGOs too have arisen to the occasion to supplement, complement, augment and collaborate with the government and private sector in reaching the deprived as well as in charting the policies for social justice. The Non-Governmental Organisations (NGOs) in their search for new and innovative ways of participation has brought forth different approaches, levels and tools of participation

## Concept of Voluntary Organisations

When any group combines for a given purpose, even if the group consists of only two persons or more, we have the psychic fundamentals of organisation, plus the principle, which must underline all associated effort. Two men unite their strength to move some object that is too heavy or bulky to be moved by one; here we have an associated effort, which is synonymous with organisation, and likewise, coordination, the first principle that underlines all such effort. Organisation is the form of every human association for the attainment of a common purpose. Organisations are social units (or human groupings) deliberately constructed and reconstructed to seek specific goals. Individuals are surrounded by organizations from the day they are born to the day that they die. The term organization is used to mean institutions such as hospitals, schools, factories, offices, the armed forces, and so on. In fact in modern society it is impossible to escape from the influence of organisations of one type or another.

According to Beveredge (1949), 'A voluntary organisation is an organization which, whether its workers are paid or unpaid, is initiated and governed by its own members without external control'. Smith and Freedman (1972) defines voluntary organisation as 'structured, formally organized, relatively permanent, secondary groupings as opposed to less structured, informal, ephemeral or primary groupings, identified by the presence of offices filled through some established procedures periodic, scheduled meetings, qualifying criteria for membership, and some formalized division and specialization of labour'.

The concept of Non-Governmental Organisation (NGO) has come from the voluntary sector. Certain times both the terms are used synonymously. According to Marshall (1996), the voluntary sector cannot be seen just in terms of service provision, but includes distinct (sub) sectors such as informal cares, self-help and community activity, and action that have a religious motivation ('missionary') as well as organized voluntary service. Voluntary action can move across sectors and much of the purpose of such action is to generate change in other sectors, although it also serves to preserve as well as change. The common element to all voluntary organizations is that they serve as mediators between the individual and the state, both holding society together and lubricating it for social change. This study uses the terms Voluntary Organisations and NGOs synonymously.

The private and statutory sectors are usually more clearly defined, while the voluntary sector tends to be seen in negative or residual terms according to what it is not; that is not for profit and not statutory. The concept of market failure or contract failure explains the need for a complementary sector. The welfare state concept gives the statutory sector dominance in this respect. Within the welfare State model the role of the voluntary sector is seen as dealing with what might be termed statutory failure, mopping up the needs of minority interest group, extending provision beyond the basic, filling gaps, providing a more personalized approach a safety—not below the safety net, as it were. This whole way of viewing the sector is deficient.

According to the National Convention on the Role of Voluntary Organisations in health care in India, a voluntary organisation is 'a social service and developmental institution motivated to meet the needs of the most disadvantaged in society, either through direct services to the people or through facilitative/indirect services to other voluntary organisation on government; non-profit making and not undertaken to be fully funded for its maintenance, directly or indirectly by the government' (Rana, 2001).

## Characteristics of NGOs

Rana (2001), gives the following as the characteristic of and specialities of NGOs. They are voluntary, have a legal status, independent in nature and flexible. They are quicker in decision-making, they are non-profit oriented, not self serving, hold high motivation, enjoy freedom in work, are value driven, catalytic in their role and people centred. The basic features of voluntary organisation are: (1) It is registered under an appropriate Act to give a corporate status to a group of individuals, so that they get a legal personality and an individual liability may give place to group liability. (2) It has an administrative structure and a duly constituted managing executive committee. (3) It has definite aims and objects and programmes in fulfilment of those. (4) It is an organisation initiated and governed by its own members on democratic principles without any external control.

The term 'volunteering' is often used to services provided free by individuals working through voluntary organisation, generally of a philanthropic (secular or religious) kind. One could interpret 'volunteering' in much wider way, however, and see it as covering any action that individuals choose to contribute for the greater social good, through whatever means or sector they prefer.

**Table 2.1:** Marshall (1996) provides the sectors of organized action

| *Sector* | *Criterion for allocation of action* | *Sources of Control* | *Contribution to Social change* |
|---|---|---|---|
| Private | Economic: Who can pay | Market | Does not alter Inequality |
| Statutory Redistribution | Legal: Who is entitled | Government | Systemic |
| Religious | Moral: Who is seen as deserving | Religious group | Local Redistribution |
| Philanthropic | Moral: Who is seen as deserving | Providers | Local Redistribution |
| Community | Political: Who can mobilize | Beneficiaries | Empowerment |
| Informal Community | Social: Who belongs | Culture | Reproduce |

Generally, voluntary agencies and non-official organisations are not necessarily voluntary. Voluntary organizations are spontaneous in their origin whereas non-official agencies may also be government sponsored. A unique feature of voluntary agency is that it stimulates voluntary action among the served community and progressively involves enlightened individuals belonging to the served community in the higher echelons of its decision-making machinery.

## Types of NGOs

For Chandra (2001), the term NGO embraces a wide variety of organisations. They include Voluntary Organisations (VOs) that pursue a social mission driven by a commitment to shared values. Public Service Contractors (PSCs) are those functions as market oriented non-profit businesses serving public purposes. People's Organisations (POs) that represent their members, interests, have leadership accountable to members, and are substantially self-reliant. Government Non-governmental Organisations

(GONGOs) are creations of government and serve as instruments of government policy. (The term Private Voluntary Organization (PVO), common in the United States, is largely synonymous with NGO).

Singh (2002), classified voluntary agencies into six categories based on the approaches they adopt and the priority they give. (1) *Charity*—Giving food, clothing, medicine, alms, in cash and in kind, land building, etc. (2) *Welfare*—providing facilities for education, health, drinking water, roads, communication, etc. (3) *Relief*—Responsibility to call of duties during natural calamities like floods, drought, earthquakes and manmade calamities like refugee influx, ravages of war, etc. (4) *Rehabilitation*—continuing and follow up of the work in areas struck by calamities and starting activities that are durable in nature. (5) *Services*—Building up infrastructure in depressed backward areas. (6) *Development of Human Beings*—Conscious raising, awaking, raising conscience, organising, recording of priorities to suit social justice; redeeming the part and opening doors for opportunities to the oppressed and the exploited.

***Strategies of NGOs***

The critical development issue for the present is not growth; it is transformation. Our collective future depends on achieving a transformation of our institutions, our technology, our values, and our behaviour consistent with our ecological and social realities. The vision is gaining clarity and followers through an evolutionary, experience-based process that involves countless individuals and organizations. The movement of which this vision is a product, however, remains incident and lacks a defining self-awareness. Getting to the twentyfirst century is intended to contribute toward strengthening this identity and self-awareness. The NGOs need to embrace this vision and devise strategies to attain them.

Rana (2001), gives light on the strategies of NGOs in the development process dividing them into four stages (Table 2.2).

**Table 2.2:** Strategies of Development Oriented NGOs: Four Generations

| | *GENERATIONS* | | | |
|---|---|---|---|---|
| | First | Second | Third | Fourth |
| | Relief and Welfare | Community Development | Sustainable Systems Development | Peoples Movements |
| Problem Definition | Shortage | Local Inertia | Institutional and Policy Constraints | Inadequate Mobilizing Vision |
| Time Frame | Immediate | Project Life | Ten to Twenty Years | Indefinite Future |
| Scope | Individual or Family | Neighbourhood or Village | Religion or nation | National or Global |
| Chief Actors | NGO | NGO plus community | All Relevant Public and Private Institutions | Loosely Defined Networks of People and Organizations |
| NGO Role | Doer | Mobiliser | Catalyst | Activist/Educator |
| Management Orientation | Logistics management | Project management | Strategic Management | Coalescing and Energizing Self-Managing Networks |
| Development Education | Starving Children | Community Self-Help | Constraining Policies and Institutions | Spaceship Earth |

## NGOs in India

India has a long history and tradition of volunteerism. The establishment of Friend-in-Need Society in Madras in 1858, is one of the earliest traces of voluntary action in the modem era. The Christian missionaries imparted relief and rehabilitation services and adopted education and health care activities.

The voluntary movements in India grew with the emergence of various religious social reform movements like Brahmo Samaj, Arya Samaj, Ram Krishna Mission, etc. That followed the struggle for independence. During this period, the voluntary efforts were characterized by mass political action or achievement of the goal of independence under the leadership of Mahatma Gandhi and other national leaders. Gandhiji's call to popularize traditional handicrafts, khadi and village industries, gave a new dimension to the voluntary efforts. Many voluntary organisations like, All India Spinners Association (1925) and All India Village Industries Association (1934) were active in this era.

The occurrence of frequent floods, droughts, famines and other natural calamities during the 1950s and 1960s, prompted massive voluntary action in the field of welfare, relief and rehabilitation. During the pre-independence era, however, there were only a few charitable and social welfare groups and missionaries and they operated on a limited scale and were restricted only to few areas. In the post-independence era, the voluntary movements gained momentum and the existing voluntary organisations (VOs) started diversifying and broad basing their welfare activities and more and more organisations emerged in India.

The foundations of the contemporary voluntary agency were created in the pre-independence period, some of them associated with the social reform movements of the late nineteenth century, largely concerned with educational and cultural matters and only tangentially with the question of poverty. Christian missionary groups established network of hospitals, schools and welfare services for the poor in the first half of the twentieth century. A third tradition was the Gandhi an approach, which combined social reform with the village development activities (Rindell *et al.*, 1995).

A new dimension was given to voluntary efforts during the 1960s and 1970s under the influence of various social, economic and political movements, e.g., Sarvodaya Movement, Youth Movements, etc. Today, the changing social and economic milieu has forced the Indian VOs to shift their areas of action. They have diversified their activities and are more professional in their approach. The process of networking is also seen among the Indians as was never before (Chandra, 2001).

Nevertheless some networks have been established in the State level to present a common front in negotiations with government over legislation and policy formulation. Some NGOs have sought to form networks with specific advocacy objectives very recently such as trying to encourage the government to introduce a guaranteed employment programme nationally and push for one-third reservation of seats for women in the Parliament.

The Community Development Programmes, Panchayati Raj system, and Cooperative system adopted by the government to encourage people's participation and to improve the condition of the poor, have largely failed to achieve their goals. The poor could not participate effectively or benefit substantially from these governments sponsored programmes. The failure of government to reach the poor effectively, gave way to the rapid growth and expansion of new movements in the country. The crucial role of VOs in certain vital sectors of development is well recognised by the Government of India (GoI) ever since the First Five Year Plan. The GoI has taken a cooperative stance towards the voluntary organisations and support their efforts. It gives not only wide recognition to voluntary organisations but also promotes, stimulates and develops NGOs by providing them assistance (both financial and technical) in furtherance of shared objectives in the successive Five Year Plan periods.

Since the Sixth Five Year Plan, more emphasis has been laid on the promotion of the VOs (both formal and informal), in order to secure people's participation in its various programmes. The Government's commitments to promotion of voluntary effort is being reflected in the creation of agencies such as the Central Social Welfare Board (CSWB) in 1953; and the Council for Advancement of People's Action and Rural Technology (CAPART) in 1986. The CSWB has a working relationship with voluntary agencies. Similarly, the CAPART aims at encouraging, promoting and assisting voluntary agencies for an effective implementation of rural development programmes in the country.

The Government has laid stress on greater involvement of voluntary agencies in various rural development programmes. As the Seventh Five Year Plan Document (1985-90), states, "serious efforts would be made to involve voluntary agencies in various development programmes, particularly, in the planning and implementation of programmes of rural development", The Eighth Five Year Plan Document (1992-97), also conforms to this policy (Chandra, 2001).

The fundamental objectives of NGO activity in rural India are poverty alleviation and the empowerment of the poor, primarily through small scale development projects. Some NGOs have chosen to tackle these symptoms of poverty manifested in low standards, ill health, poor sanitation and inferior housing by means of social welfare programmes. Some others concentrate on enhancing the asset position and income earning potential of the poor through land improvement schemes, credit and skill training. An alternative approach has been of NGOs for poor people to demand resources from the sate or to challenge injustice and exploitation (Rindell, *et al.,* 1995).

Rindell (1995), observes that NGOs in India can be grouped into five categories according to their scale of operations and location of their head office—

(i) Large indigenous NGOs working in several States in different parts of the country or working in most districts of one State.
(ii) Medium sized indigenous NGOs working in large number of villages in one or two districts of one State.
(iii) Small indigenous NGOs working in a group of villages in one locality (the most common type).
(iv) Large international NGOs within the country providing funding and support to indigenous NGOs.
(v) Small international NGOs working directly in one or two countries.

Funding mechanisms fall into four categories. The first is where the donor operates exclusively through intermediary agency in India, which is responsible for identifying suitable projects, liaison with partners, monitoring, and evaluating their activities. The second type is the consortium model favoured by the churches, where the donor agencies pool their funds, usually in the form of Block grants, which are then distributed by an intermediary agency. The third approach is that favoured by Oxfam, Save the Children Fund and NOVIB, all of which have in the country the Indian nationals forming part of the parent organisation and performing a role similar to that of an intermediary agency. The fourth model does not involve an intermediary agency and relations between donor and recipient operate on a one to one basis. Project is submitted directly to the funding agency, which processes the applications in its head office.

Estimates of the number of NGOs active in rural development in India range from not less than 1,00,000 to several hundred thousand depending upon the type of classification is used. Nearly 20,0000 organizations are registered with the Ministry of Home Affairs for foreign funding, although the list does not distinguish between religious organisation (such as mosques and temples management committees) commercial bodies and voluntary agencies; only half of these fall into the NGO category.

Recent estimates suggest that the amount of foreign funds coming into the country for use by NGOs each year is in the region of Rs. 9 bn. (US$ 520 m.), up from Rs. 5 bn in the mid 1980s. In quantitative terms, this is equivalent to approximately 20 per cent of official aid flows, which stood at $24 bn in 1991. A further Rs. 500—700m is provided by the government. When individual and corporate donations are added in, an annual income figure of Rs. 10 bn would seem a reasonable estimate of the total available resources, although this does not take into account unofficial payments or contributions in kind by project beneficiaries (Rindell, 1995).

The volume of aid channelled to India by the bilateral agencies account for nearly one-third of the total foreign aid (i.e. rupees 425 billion by 1994), while the multilateral aid accounts for more than half of the total volume of aid. The external resources channelled to the NGO sector through the government was nearly rupees 32 billion by 1994, i.e., over seven per cent of the external aid to India.

**Table 2.3:** NGOs in India receiving Foreign Aid during 1990-91 to 1993-94

| *Year* | *Number of NGOs* | *Total Foreign Aid (in million rupees)* |
|---|---|---|
| 1990-91 | 9,316 | 954.7 |
| 1991-92 | 9,012 | 14,121.3 |
| 1992-93 | 10,201 | 15,843.0 |
| 1993-94 | 10,963 | 18,657.0 |

*Source: The Week,* September 15, 1996.

According to Foreign Contribution (Regulation) Act (FCRA) estimates, there are about 16,000 voluntary agencies in India, which received foreign aid during 1992-93. The total foreign aid received by the NGOs of the country amounted to rupees 15,842 million. Half of the total aid is contributed, by USA and Germany. The State of Tamil Nadu is the leading State in India that received more than 17 per cent (i.e. 2,728 rupees million) of the total foreign aid in the voluntary sector during 1992-93. The other States and Union territories which received more than 10 per cent of the total foreign aid in the voluntary sector during the same period include Delhi, Maharashtra, Karnataka and Kerala.

## Non-Governmental Organizations in Development

The role of Non-Governmental Organizations (NGOs) in the development of the nation is increasingly accepted in the modern world. Their activities range from providers of the basic facilities to social action. The role of NGOs in the progress of society has been undoubtedly established in the last few decades. The NGOs enjoy a comparative advantage than the Government sector, thanks to the small geographical areas and targeted interventions, in evolving new and innovative ideas. NGOs have contributed highly to the advancement of participatory approaches in different parts of the world. The efforts of them in bringing participation in the forefront of development have influenced the governments to adopt participatory approaches.

A number of NGOs throughout the world are giving attention to the definition and projection of a people centred development vision that embraces the transformation agenda. This vision looks to justice, sustainability and inclusiveness as the defining principles of authentic development. It views development as a people's movement more than as a foreign funded government project. It looks to government to enable the people to develop themselves. It seeks a synthesis of the change objectives of the environmental, human rights, consumer protection, women's and peace movements. It seeks new human consciousness in which the more nurturing, enabling and conserving dimensions of female consciousness gain ascendance over the more aggressive, exploitative and competitive dimensions of male consciousness that have so long dominated the social and economic life of human societies.

The NGO movements in Asia, Africa and Latin America grew rapidly during the 1970s and 1980s, and they arose mainly out of social conflicts and tensions, the need to respond more effectively to economic crisis situations, and/or the failure of governments to deal with the growing socio-economic problems. For example, NGOs in Bangladesh were formed during and after the War of Independence in 1971. Bangladesh Rural Advancement Committee was established to respond to the refugee problems which arose due to the war.

There is widespread agreement among development practitioners, government officials and foreign donors that NGOs play an important role in helping to alleviate rural poverty in India, complementary to that of government, both in terms of providing additional resources and in making government programmes more effective. With the introduction of economic planning and major developmental programmes, the NGOs began to supplement government efforts, undertook developmental programmes along with their traditional welfare and relief activities.

## Critique of NGOs

The role of NGOs has not been free from criticism, especially in facing the challenges of globalization. According to Pearce (2000), the failures of development can no longer be attributed solely to the inability of the governments, institutions and people in charge of implementing it. In fact, if they had been successful in fulfilling the promises they made to their people, and had there been enough money and resources to bring about the development of all the so called underdeveloped countries of the world to the level of the most advanced, the resulting deadlocks and tensions would perhaps have taken an even more dramatic turn.

To what extent have development NGOs succumbed to the pressures and incentives to pick up the social cost of neo liberal restructuring, and thus enabled multilateral and governmental institutions to avoid breaking with their neo liberal faith by recreating welfare states. While the discourse of these institutions has become notably more socially aware and human centred, the underlying progressive philosophy of marketed globalization has not been questioned. NGOs were not unable to offer the solution to the social cost of economic restructuring. Criticisms of NGO have focused on their technical deficiency, their lack of accountability, and their excessively politicised and critical character. This failure has undermined their credibility among the technocrats within donor institutions, who demanded rapid and measurable outputs from investments in NGO sector.

The NGOs have privileged the vision of western donor agencies and turned 'civil society' into a project than a process. In other words, by assuming that there is no debate around what we would like civil society to be and assuming that it is an unproblematic and empirically observable given, whose purpose is unquestionably to build democracy and foster development, the vision of powerful and well resources donors predominates. Failure to clarify their own position means that many NGOs end up simply implementing that vision on the donor's behalf.

Nevertheless, the parameters of debate are clearer now. This is after years in which many NGOs of North and South have more or less reluctantly let themselves be led and/or influenced official donor agendas and techno efficiency determinism. Official donors have reached out to NGOs while also pushing the neo-liberal restructuring that many believe is part of the problem faced by the poor, not the solution.

Development of NGOs in the poor countries need to reestablish public confidence in order to persuade donors to continue channel funds through them. They identify four areas of concern as following. One is the failure of NGOs to develop accountability within their own countries rather the accountability to wealthy foreign organization. Second the need for internal reform and mechanisms to 'institutionalize suspicion' within NGO that are undergoing structural growth, and thus regain trust and confidence in the eyes of the public government and donors. Third, the need for NGOs to pre-empt the often intrusive and inappropriate formal, quantitative performance evaluation favoured by donors by developing quality ratings their own and the fourth, the need to overcome the tendency for small NGOs to compete with each other, by seeking economies of scale through collectively provided services within the NGO sector.

However, the Global North and South have emphatically accepted the private public partnership and the role of NGOs in development. The various policies of Government of India has accepted the position of NGOs and given advancing roles in the development spheres. But the NGOs too need to listen to criticisms as well as do self-reflections to consistently improvise their services.

# 3

# Participatory Approaches in Development

Several ideas, methods and practices have contributed to development of humankind at different times in history. All of them seek to provide justice and equity to every member of this world. Participation has become a strong norm in development in last forty years. The players in the development sector have embraced participation as an important catalyst for development. Participation seeks informed and active inclusion of all the stakeholders in the process of development. However, there have been different meaning attributed to it and multitude of interpretations in its realms.

## Participation as Defined and as Understood

There are different thoughts on participation which one way or other complement each other. Generally understood, participation is a process through which stakeholders influence and share control over development initiatives and the decisions and the resources which affect them. This is a very broad understanding on participation, which comprises international, national and local scenario.

Bhose (2003), defines participation as a process wherein people involve themselves in planning, decision-making and carrying out activities, projects, movements or whatsoever towards betterment with or without external support and sustain the same as individuals, peoples organisation and social institutions.

Uphooff (2003), opines that participation includes people's involvement in decision-making process, in implementing programmes... their sharing in the benefits of development programmes and their involvement in the efforts to evaluate such programmes.

Participation should include the notions of contributing, influencing, sharing, or redistributing power and of control, resources, benefits, knowledge, and skills to be gained through beneficiary involvement in decision-making. Participation is a voluntary process by which people, including the disadvantaged (in income, gender, caste or education), influence or control the decisions that affect them. According to Saxena (1996), the essence of participation is exercising voice and choice, and developing the human, organizational and management capacity to solve problems as they arise in order to sustain the improvements.

Santhanam (1993), defines participation as commitment on the part of the individual towards all forms of actions by which the individual can 'take part' or 'play a role' in the operation without being conscious of any socio-economic barriers to achieve certain common goals in a group situation.

Participation involves a process aimed at social equity in the long run. Korten (2001), states that participation is a process by which the members of society increase their personal and institutional capacities to mobilize and manage their resources to produce sustainable and justly distributed improvements in their quality of life consistent with their own aspirations.

Talking on civic participation, a term of recent origin, Kashyap (2008), states that civic participation refers to the space constructed by citizens to work next to their authorities in the decision-making, policy formulation and implementation process. It refers to the execution and monitoring of governmental activities with the purpose of improving the quality of life of the population. It also contributes to the public agenda, to the fight against corruption and to the development of higher living standards. Civic participation is regarded as the process by which citizen concerns needs, values, exceptions and problems are taken into account into the governmental decision-making process. It has three interrelated elements. (1) Open to transparent government;

(2) Constant and persistent flow of information from government to its citizens and *vice versa*; and (3) Efficient ways of informing the citizens about their roles and responsibilities to participate as equal partners.

Any operational definition of people's participation has to capture the range and nuances of the concept. First of all, the term 'people' needs to be clarified. It need not necessarily denote the entire community, for such a community could be heterogeneous in its socio-economic mix. It indicates a homogeneous group of people hitherto excluded from the development process, who share certain socio-economic characteristics. As far as a development project is concerned, people below poverty line, whom the project calls beneficiaries, are the primary stakeholders or partners, in the development process. In addition, people above poverty line, within the community, and collaborating with the project, whom the project calls benefactors have significant role in the overall development of the area. Because of this, the beneficiaries and benefactors participation could be of different degrees and quality.

Participation is also used to refer to a desirable form of involvement over a range of services and process, such as planning. It can be viewed as an end in itself, as a way of discovering how decisions and plans are likely to affect those most concerned, or a way of establishing a new power base. Schemes to encourage participation may take a number of forms of neighbourhood councils, adding consumers to decision-making bodies, developing responsibilities to groups or committees of consumers, recognizing particular groups or consultation purposes, or improving the flow of information through surveys and meetings. One major problem, of course, concerns the relationship between participation in these forms and the participative form of government called representative democracy (Sharma, 1992).

Participation carries multiple views in its perception and application. For instance, Karl Deutsch, while viewing participation as a psychosocial phenomenon, underscored its importance in the planning process in development (Arora, 1990). For Deutsch, participation denotes a technique for setting goals, choosing priorities and deciding what resources too commit to goal treatment. Such a process would assume the prevalence of genuine and active participation as against symbolic a passive participation in the decision-making system. Active participation would not simply ratify, but in fact influence administrative behaviour and the output of the official action. This way of looking at participation helps in conceptually analyzing particular development programmes in terms of active-passive participation. Nevertheless, it runs into difficulties when the issue of actually ensuring people's participation is raised. Deutsch suggests political mobilization and socialization as methods for eliciting participation. Given the nature of political development in a majority of the developing countries, such hopes would sound rather unrealistic.

The governance and the polity of western and eastern countries also affect the nature of participation in civil society (Mishra, 1993). Attempting minimal definition of participation makes some sense in stable western democracies where the concept of equality is accepted, legitimized and most important of all, where a comprehensive network of institutions has emerged and stabilized to articulate and express the needs and aspirations of cross-section of the citizenry. However, this is not the case in most countries of the non-western world. Changing socio-political and economic conditions in these countries have created an urge among the masses for participation in shaping the world they live in. But the institutional structure that has emerged in most of these countries seems incapable for containing and channelising the urge of masses. In fact, in some of the countries such institutional structures have not been allowed to grow and peoples movement, if any, have been thwarted, controlled, or repressed by the instrumentalities of the state. However, participation and development has to take place only thorough well defined and effective institutional apparatus of the state.

Arora (1993), comments on the general and political spheres of participation. He observes that most of the writings on the subject omit references to non-conventional political behaviour, demonstrations, strikes and *morchas*—not to speak of more violent activities—are absent from most standard typologies or operationalised indices of political participation; rarely does one find any willingness to discuss these models in relation to the more conventional ones. There seems to be a pressing need for a typology of political activity which will include all acts, from voting to political acts involving physical violence.

World Conference on Agrarian Reforms and Rural Development (WCARRD, 1979), treat participation as a basic human right. It states, that participation by the people in the institutions and systems to govern their lives is a basic human right and also essential for realignment of political power in favour of disadvantaged groups and for social and economic development. Rural development strategies can realize their full potential only through the motivation, active involvement and organisation at the grassroots level of rural problem with social emphasis on the least advantaged, in conceptualizing and designing policies and programmes and increasing administrative, social and economic institution, including cooperative and other voluntary forms of organisation for implementing and evaluating them.

## Typology of Participation

People's participation could be *suo motu* or induced; induced participation can be semi-coercive as in mass mobilization, or genuinely interactive. The state and local governments, NGOs and even an animator from a communication catalyse participation. When we analyse and assess the quality of a project/ programme/activity, it implies not only the quantitative and measurable achievements, but also the benefits for the welfare and development of others.

Participation can be of three kinds—involuntary participation; transient participation motivated by self-interest; and voluntary sustainable participation. Qualitative improvement through sustainable participation is impossible without a long lasting process such that organizations are formed and in the process the ability to manage resources is raised, norms are created and the mechanisms for creating them are internalized and basic abilities needed to negotiate externally are acquired.

According to Vijayanand (1996), People's participation could be of varying intensities. The range could be summarized as:

(a) Anti-participation or Negative participation where something is imposed on people against their will by an outside agency.

(b) Zero-participation, where the people are indifferent to a programme and where the sponsoring agency does not do anything to motivate the people to participate.

(c) Information sharing, which is a basic level of participation when people have access to all information on the intended programme, which may be decided from outside.

(d) Consultation, when the suggestions of the local people are heard before the project agency makes its own decision.

(e) Consent, when the local people have to give prior approval to a course of action, which could have originated from an external source.

(f) Contribution when people voluntarily part with labour, cash or materials as a token of making a programme their own.

(g) Partnership, where the people and the development agency are coequals and the whole programme is designed after dialogue, based on consensus.

(h) Autonomous action when the people are supreme and taken the final decision with or without the presence and help of an external agency. In the case of government sponsored programmes, Autonomous action is possible in areas outside the ambit of the programme in related sectors.

According to Pretty (1995), there are seven types of community participation.

1. *Participation in Information giving*: People participate by answering questions posed by extractive researchers using questionnaire surveys or similar approaches. People do not have the opportunity to influence proceedings, as the finding of the research are neither shared nor checked for accuracy.
2. *Participation by Consultation*: People participate by being consulted, and external people listen to views. These

external professionals define both problems and solutions and may modify these in the light of people's responses.

3. *Participation for Material Incentives*: People participate by providing resources, for example, labour in return for food, cash or other material incentives. Yet people have no stake in prolonging activities when the incentives end.
4. *Functional Participation*: People participate by forming groups to meet pre-determined objectives related to the project which can involve the development or promotion of externally initiated development or promotion of internally initiated social organisation. These institutions tend to be dependent.
5. *Passive Participation*: People participate by being told what is going to happen or has already happened. It is a unilateral announcement by an administration or project management without listening to people's responses.
6. *Interactive Participation*: People participate in joint analysis, which leads to action plans and the formation of new local institutions or the strengthening of existing ones. These groups take control over local decisions and so people have a stake in maintaining structures or practices.
7. *Self Mobilisation*: People participate by taking initiative independent of external institutions to change systems. Such self-initiated mobilisation and collective action may or may not challenge existing inequitable distributions of wealth and power.

The substance of participation is, however, often ill defined, and clarification is needed regarding who is participating, how and in what. Despite the 'feel-good' factor associated with participation, it must be recognized that it is not a neutral concept, and involves a set of political issues concerning who has decision-making power and who has access to resources.

**Ladder of Participation**

Arnstein's Ladder of participation tries to classify the various levels of participation in the following category (Harper, 2000).

| | |
|---|---|
| Citizen Power | Citizen control<br>Delegated power<br>Partnership |
| Tokenism | Consultation<br>Informing<br>Placation<br>Therapy |
| Non-Participation | Manipulation |

One view of participation is getting people to agree to and go along with a project, which has already been designed for them, or to get support of a few leaders (Saxena, 1998). It must be, therefore, understood as a process by which the people are able to organize themselves and, through their own organization, are able to identify their own needs, and share in the design, implementation and evaluation of the participatory action. People are likely to participate when their benefits outweigh their costs. Nevertheless, people's participation can contribute to achievement of four main objectives; effectiveness; efficiency; empowerment; and equity. Commonality of interest may supersede other distinctions, in facilitating participation.

As people participate in making new decisions and solving problems, learning takes place. It leads to changes in attitude, behaviour, confidence, and leadership. Newly acquired knowledge is, therefore, the first outcome of participation. Empowerment is a result of participation in decision-making. An empowered person is one who can take initiative, exert leadership, display confidence, solve new problems, mobilise resources, and undertake new actions. Participation in decision-making is hypothesized to strengthen the capacity of local organization to call out activities. These three outcomes of participation-learning, empowerment, and a vibrant organization-need to be measured through observable indicators, which will vary from project to project. On the issue of when to participate, participation is an evolutionary process that gathers momentum and defies breakdown into neat, self-contained categories, except for analytical purposes.

The interpretations of participation are manifold that it encompasses the objectives of development as such. Participation is treated as collaboration and organisations basis for development. Participation leads to empowerment as well (Mohanan, 2005; Saxena, 1998).

There are numerous arguments in favour of participation (Bob, 1998): (1) Efficiency referring to efficient use of resources for development; (2) Effectiveness in the projects for rural development; (3) Self-reliance of rural poor; (4) Coverage of more people with direct influence of the development activities; (5) Sustainability referring to the continuity in the momentum of development; and (6) Equity as it allows rural poor access to resources and fairer distribution of opportunities.

## Participatory Development

Participatory development is both a means to economic development and an end in itself. As a means participatory development is supportive to policies of decentralization. As an end, it refers to a political situation within which sustainable development results from the responsible action of politically mature citizens, demonstrating solidarity and acting within the framework of democratic society

Participatory development is the process by which populations and more particularly their least member influence the decisions that affect them. This process entails several steps, one of which is that of empowerment or self-governance capability. This concept implies growing democratization; power shaped more fairly, a more developed political consciousness and better political representation of the population especially the most disadvantaged groups.

Participatory development is one of the most important approaches for realizing self reliant, sustainable development and social justice. In the so called top-down approach to development the entire process of formulating and implementing policies is carried out under the direction of developing country governments and the people tend to be put in a passive position. Participatory development is an attempt to compensate for or overcome the limitations of the top down development approach. It is an approach that enables people to acquire the skills needed to implement and coordinate the management of development projects themselves and thus reaps more of development's return.

Participation has a long history in development projects in involving people in certain aspects of planning and implementation in a programme. In the earlier programmes, initiatives in this regard distorted participation, created dependence and misleading impressions. Participatory development is a socio-economic force aiming for sustained development at the village level. There is a close link between resources (land, water, forest, mineral, etc.) and community. The community uses resources with a great deal of interaction among individuals. Allocation of resources, based on a community approach, rather than on an individualized one, adds an element of sustenance to the development process.

A participatory approach, therefore, implies a major, but not exclusive, role for local populations in allocating rights and responsibilities over resources. It may involve partnership with other interest groups at micro and macro levels, such as district line agencies, local political bodies, ministries of finance, and policy makers.

## Historical Evolution of Participatory Approaches

There has been search for alternatives, which led to the development of many novel conceptual constructs and strategies. A participatory approach has come in the changing paradigms of development strategies and inevitably affected the whole segments of development process. The concern with participation led development planners, experts and academicians to conceptually elaborate the meaning of participation and its various connotations.

It was in the 1970s, however, that the participation became the subject of elaborate research and discussion among development scholars and agencies (Arora, 1990). For instance, the Maxwell School of the Syracuse University launched the Local Revenue Administration Project to carry out research on participatory local government and rural development. Here, special emphasize was given to local level resources mobilization through the participation of the people. The rural development

Participation Project at Cornell University's centre of International studies was also deeply involved in studying the participation. The Cornell group viewed the evaluation phase as one in which participation could be fruitfully included. Notably, despite the MIT recommendations of 1969, the tendency in international development circles in the 1960s and 1970s has been to think of participation as largely confined to the output or benefit stage of the project cycle. This concern was reinforced by the new directions emphasis at USAID in the 1970s and the redistributions with growth focus at the World Bank at the same time. Both were concerned with meeting the needs of target groups like the bottom group and others concerned with USAID's office of Rural Development helped enlarge this cycle of participation to include other phases of the project.

Yet another trend discernible in the late 1970s on the issue of participatory development was the emphasize on people's participation which implied effective devolution of decision-making powers in administration and planning in favour of the people at the grassroots level, particularly in areas that affect their lives directly. Simultaneously, attention had to shift from a centralized administrative and planning process to a decentralized administrative and planning format based on people's participation. This necessarily had to depend on mobilization of the people through their own organisations. Since in many developing countries, local government institutions had evolved historically as organisations of the local people for their uplift, the question was raised if these organisations could be revamped to play a more crucial and dynamic role in promoting participatory development and administration.

For successfully implementing people centred development projects, the need is to devise institutional and administrative means for bridging the gaps indicated above. For this, many options such as the involvement of the Non-Governmental Organisations (NGOs), cooperatives and other alternatives have been tried in different countries with varying results. What has come out crystal clear is that by ignoring government institutional systems, it is difficult and inadvisable to initiate and implement people centred development in the developing nations. The flurry of activities and enthusiasm with decentralized local government systems and efforts of several developing countries to entrust the people's representatives with running the affairs of local administration are actions that raise hope that people centred development may take off the ground successfully. However, further education and training of the people in management and other skills is necessary so that they may take a more informed view of the problems of development and their place in it. Similarly, government functionaries are required to be reoriented through conscientisation and training so that they develop a positive attitude towards the people and the philosophy and strategy of people centred development.

## Participation in Action

In India, the government with the launching of the Community Development Programmes in 1952 initiated the first major Rural Development Schemes. Community Development Projects are of vital importance not so much for the natural achievement that they bring about, but much more so, because they seem to build up the community and the individuals. Apparently, community development was viewed as a social movement with active involvement of the people, aimed at all round development of the countryside. The participatory nature of government programme have generated from this movement onwards.

Muraleedharan (2006), suggests that for effective implementation of the participatory development programmes, one should not view participation a merely an input to the implementation of the programme but as an underlining operational principle, which should underpin all activities. It is to be regarded as intrinsic to the programmes for development and not simply as an activity that is used from time to time to whip up beneficiary interests. Participation in development offers a chance for the people to participate in such type of development activities and probably it may seek to make the more common, top down and technocratic approach to the project development more participatory by evolving some frameworks to include the efforts of people in one or other stage of it. Participatory development implies a radical change in the project management and it is far different from simply adjusting the project planning cycle or allowing for a degree of local involvement.

The State of Kerala had been a torchbearer in carrying out the participatory approaches in local governance with people's plan campaign since the Ninth Five Year Plan within the Panchayati Raj System. A study by Muraleedharan (2006), reveals that there has been continuous increase in the female participation of Gram Sabha, the basic unit of civic administration. In the urban area, the participation of women has exceeded the targets while the target in rural areas fell short of it at meagre percentage. Kerala experiment offers the right perspective of gendering governance and empowering women by providing many opportunities for poor women to participate in the political and economic process of planning at the local level from identification of local development problems to the implementation of development projects in various capacities. It has led to changes in the role of people, in particular women, but also there has been the change in the role played by the official machinery in the planning.

Vaidyanathan (2001), points out that the involvement of people in decision-making does not ensure that they will be willing to take up the responsibility of management for several reasons. Firstly, they need to be convinced that programmes like watershed development will make a significant difference to the overall livelihood opportunities and incomes of community. The communities know much about conditions of local resources and problems experienced in their utilization. But locally available knowledge and expertise needed to make use of the resources to maximum collective advantage is generally inadequate. If the entire cost is borne by the government or other external agency, the sense of stake on the part of the community in the project is apt to be weak. It is, therefore, important to insist on the community sharing, in cash or in kind, a substantial part of costs of the development. The larger its contribution the greater will be the incentive for the community to address seriously the task of maintenance and sharing of benefits and costs.

The participatory natural resource management has led to effective use and protection of the scarce natural resources and providing perennial sources of life support to people around. The community participation in construction and managing check dams and use of water through lift irrigation has transferred the local ecosystem of thirty-seven tribal villages in Vasndi taluk of Gujarat's Valsad district (Singh, 2005). Cropping patterns, income, employment and even the social systems have undergone remarkable changes. The villages are now very energetically engaged in the orchards, fodder crops, vegetable and fuelwood management. They were supported by the Bhartiya Agro Industries Foundation (BAIF) a Pune base NGO.

Another case is of Hivare, a village about thirty-five kilometres away from Pune. The villagers used to migrate to cities in the barren rabi season. The participatory natural resource management changed the entire landscape of the village. The people collectively in association with government and voluntary organisations constructed checkdams which raised the ground water level, slowed down erosion and helped to increase crop yield. VANARAI, a Pune based NGO motivates and provides practical assistance to villagers.

The participatory approaches have been followed in various government projects as well. The National Rural Employment Guarantee (NREG) programme implemented in Andhra Pradesh had adopted the participatory approaches in it. In the planning stage of the project people attended *en masse* in the Gram Sabha (Bob, 2008). The poor people participated more as that was the forum used for the registration for the work. The more number of women participated from the labour localities and middle class but not from upper class due to cultural norms.

The government department executed the work without contractors. One of the literate workers involved in measurement of the work and in the calculation of wages. The rural folk participated in the implementation stage by providing labour on payment of wages. On the benefit receiving end of the project, the poor directly benefited with the provision of work at the minimum wage, whatever, the nature of work. In the evaluation stage of the project, there were a number of informal evaluation meetings conducted with the participation of the local people in general and workers in particular. They were held at the site itself and discussed all the aspects of the work including the usefulness and problems in the execution of the work. A theoretical analysis of participation finds this project has followed the incremental, manipulative, participatory and anti-participatory levels of Midgley's typology of participation.

**Participatory Approaches in International Arena**

Gupta (2006), finds out that decentralized governance is effectively strengthened and rendered more accountable when participation is encouraged, facilitated and institutionalized. Communities, neighbourhoods and individuals can play a crucial role in ensuring that local government responds to their needs by participating in the planning and implementation of activities and projects that affect their lives. This eventually affects the level of human development they maintain.

More effective participation of civil society and the private sector in local development process that is managed by local government is often cited as one of the more important reasons for success in decentralization imitative. In all the cases he undertook for study participation has played a significant role. These range from consultation on education issues (Jordan) to involvement in decision-making (Brazil and Honduras) and implementation of community projects (India).

In the Honduras case, all the communities in the municipality of Sinuapa have organized neighbourhood associations. These coordinate their plans and activities among themselves and with municipal authorities through Municipal Development Council (CODEM), the coordinating municipal level body. Plans submitted to CODEM are supported by communities not only through their involvement in decision-making, but also through the launching of specific projects.

The Indian case, involving the rural local government of Jamunia a Tanak Grama Panchayat, in Madhya Pradesh particularly focuses on community level participation. In this case, efforts were made to involve the local residents in a wide variety of activities from which they had formerly excluded or in which they had been only marginally involved. Other instance of community participation included both labour and financial contributions by residents to the construction of a village drainage system, raising funds within the community for a teachers' salary, volunteering to teach illiterate adults and organizing a house to house campaign to encourage women to attend literacy classes.

The Philippines local government cases, where civil society is very strong are also impressive cases of local participation. For example, the Balilihan Country Action Programme (BCAP) used *puroks* (neighbourhood association) extensively. Neighbourhood volunteers have worked in each of the seven sectoral programmes they conduct. Prominent members of the community have donated small lots of land for neighbourhood kiosks, which are sued as community centres.

Participation has taken different forms in Poland and the degree of citizens' involvement has varied across the various municipalities. The municipality of Tarnovo, for instance formed citizens committees, which have played an important role in the financing and implementation of municipal infrastructure projects. In Bilgoraj, the voluntary local committees are involved in the development of infrastructure, including water supply and sewage systems, street lighting and construction.

In the Brazil case, some community participation was inherent in Belo Horizonte use of the health care committees and community activism was encouraged by the committees. In both cases in Jordan there was some level of local participation in the educational development committees. SKAA in Pakistan delegated selected decision-making authority to the community, and the community monitors the work of contractors. In the case of Jinja in Uganda, the market vendor association encouraged participation in making decisions about the market. The above quoted studies points to the significance of participatory approach in the civic administration and development process in different countries.

The analysis and interpretation of participation in different dimensions assumes the active involvement of people from every sphere in decision-making that affect their life. Participation *per se* is a change strategy and empowers the stakeholders. It is this merit of participation that the Government as well as the Non-Governmental agencies initiates participation in the planning, implementing, monitoring and evaluation of development programmes. Participation has acclaimed a significant role in the development efforts in different parts of the world. The NGOs have been in the forefront to initiate grassroot changes through participatory practices and experiment participatory approaches in non-conventional fields.

# 4

# Concept and Application of PRA

Participatory Rural Appraisal (PRA) is one of the most widely recognized and established methodology of participatory development process. It has undergone several historical changes in its approaches, methods and applicability. PRA, the brainchild of the British rural development expert Prof. Robert Chambers is being extensively used in appraisal, analyses and action. It helps to analyse the problems of the community in their perspective, prioritise them and present an action plan with community participation. PRA has been defined as 'a family of approaches and methods to enable people to share, enhance and analyse their knowledge of life and conditions to plan, act, to monitor and evaluate'. It is now a philosophy and a way of life which stresses self critical awareness and commitment of the poor, weak and vulnerable.

## Evolution of PRA

Looking into the history of past three decades we come across five methodological and conceptual streams which directly and indirectly contribute to a confluence PRA. They are Participative action reflection research, Agro Ecosystem Analysis, Applied Anthropology, Field Research on farming systems and Rapid Rural Appraisal (RRA). Moreover, as an approach in development, PRA has been influenced by several factors like traditions, approaches, methods understandings, etc., of different branches of social and natural science and practices in the world.

Rapid Rural Appraisal developed in 1970s by conducting on site study by a multi-disciplinary team, which uses simple non-standard methods and local people's knowledge to elicit, analyze and evaluate information. It is suitable for evaluation diagnosing and identifying rural situation, particularly when quick action in a project region for analyzing a special problem for resolving conflict or for focusing on certain tools of monitoring and evaluation. RRA has really enabled the outsiders to gain information and insight from rural people in a more cost effective and less time consuming manner. However, RRA also remained as exploitative and extractive as very little was given back to the rural people. As the term depicts it was rapid and the outsiders' interest of data collection dominated it.

Whereas, in the mid-1980s the term "Participation" got recognition in RRA. In 1985 in the Khon Khaen international conference the term participation was used in connection with RRA. In 1988, Participatory RRAs were listed by the IIED (International Institute of Environment and Development, University of Sussex, UK) term alongwith exploratory RRAs, topical RRAs and monitoring RRAs (Mukherjee, 2002). Later the term PRA was widely recognized with its strategic change in the methodology and approach.

By mid-1996, activities described as PRA were being practiced in perhaps 100 countries and there are more than 30 PRA networks all over the world. Now not only NGOs and government departments but also training institutes and universities were increasingly using PRA methods and approaches. PRA has developed to Participatory Learning and Action (PLA) which gives emphasis on empowerment, action and learning from them.

PRA stresses that those actually affected should assume an active role in analyzing their condition and evaluating the result. It is the way of enabling local people to analyze their living conditions, share outcomes and to plan their activities. It concentrates on strengthening decision-making abilities to local communities while bringing about changes in the attitudes of outsiders regarding their role in the process. The focus is on learning from with and through community members. PRA has found unquestionable reputation in development process ensuring participation (Mukherjee, 2004).

**Foundations of PRA**

The three foundations of PRA are behaviour, sharing and methods. Behaviour includes approach and attitude to hand over the stick in the belief that people can teach you. The worker is to sit down, relax, embrace errors and use one's own judgments always. They share their knowledge with each other and with study team. All share experiences, collective learning and collective presentations. Use of multiple methods like interview, ranking, observe, comparing, diagrams, etc., is followed in PRA (Kumar, 1996).

**The Principles PRA**

1. *A Reversal of Learning*: The emphasis on learning from the local people and gaining insight into the social, economic, political, technical, physical fields form the indigenous knowledge of the people.
2. *Learning Progressively*: By using appropriate and flexible methods in a sequential manner, instead of a blueprint learning programme; the participants will logically interact in the collective search.
3. *Offsetting Bias*: Listening not lecturing, probing not passing on, seeking out those who are marginalised, isolated and remote, learning their concerns, and priorities, comfortable with the limited convenience, giving priority to the convenient time and place of the participants.
4. *Optimising the Learning*: It is also known as principle of optimal ignorance, i.e., not learning more than necessary, not measuring what need not be measured
5. *Triangulating or Cross-Checking*: This is to validate the data and information. It is done at three levels: by changing the methods of learning; by changing the sources of information; and by changing the Constitution of the learning team.
6. *Complexity and Diversity*: This is to seek complex and diverse information. It is looking for and learning from exceptions and contradictions. It goes beyond cross checking or triangulation.

7. *Handing over the Stick*: This principle builds confidence in the capability of people becoming facilitators—facilitating investigation, analysis, presentation and learning by local people themselves so that they generate and own the outcomes.
8. *Self Critical Awareness*: It aims at continuous and critical examination of one's own behaviour by embracing error, learning from failures and mistakes in the process of learning, interaction and sharing.
9. *Personal Responsibility*: The learners are responsible for all the findings, learning and outcomes and not relying on any other authority or manuals or on rigid rules.
10. *Sharing*: Sharing of information ideas and knowledge between local people, facilitators, bureaucrats, elected leaders, experts, professionals and gaining insight for planning and action.
11. *Learning by Doing*: Most of the information, knowledge and ideas are generated by doing, performing and strictly focusing on the interactions, participation, application of methods, etc. This is the principle of do it oneself in the group and own up the findings.

**Tools of PRA**

One of the important features of PRA is the visually appealing, easily comprehensible and people friendly tools of it. The important tools of PRA are the following (Praxis, 1998).

1. *Social Mapping*: People make map of their locality by using colours and locally available materials and indicate the important institutions, roads and other details of their community. It gives a clear picture of a particular community very quickly.
2. *Resource Mapping*: This is drawing and colouring on the ground by rural people with the minimum of interference by outsiders of the details of resources in their community often about a particular sector like agriculture.
3. *Seasonal Calendars*: This tool explores seasonal constraints

and opportunities by diagramming changes in the months throughout the year. Seasonal calendars can be drawn in linear fashion with 12 months to show a typical year or 8 months to illustrate changes between years; or can be drawn in a circle.

4. *Daily Routine Analyses*: It explores daily patterns of activity through profiles and routines, chart for each hour of the day typical activities, amount of effort, time taken and location of work. It is used to compare for different people, profiles and routines for different seasons.
5. *Semi-Structured Interview*: This is guided interviewing and listening in which only some of the question and topics are predetermined, and questions arise during the interview. Using a guide or checklist the multi-disciplinary team poses open ended questions and probes topics as they arise.
6. *Key Informant Interview*: Ask the experts in the community on a particular phenomenon under study. Put together a series of interviews with key informants of a different stage of a process.
7. *Time Line*: A history of major recollected events in a community with approximates dates are collected through discussion and simultaneously recorded. It throws light to the historical evolution of the community or changes in a particular sector like agriculture over a period of time.
8. *Chapati (or Venn) Diagrams*: This includes use of circles to represent people, groups and institutions. People arrange these to represent degree of relationship with various institutions. While the size of the circle represents the significance of the institution, the distance they place it from their community shows their functional relationship with those institutions.
9. *Participatory Diagramming*: This is making, drawing and colouring on the ground by rural people with the minimum of interference and instruction by outsiders on particular matters like housing. Social and resource mapping also fall under the category of participatory mapping.

10. *Pairwise Ranking and Scoring*: In pairwise ranking items of interest are compared pair by pair, informants being asked which is preferred of two and why.
11. *Matrix Ranking*: Matrix ranking and scoring takes criteria for the rows in a matrix and items columns, and people fill in the boxes for each row. This helps in reaching a consensus on decisions.
12. *Inflow Outflow Diagram*: This is representation by the people on ground, of the resources, goods and services flowing to the community and those flowing out of the community. They are represented by the materials available in the locality.
13. *Cases and Stories*: Brief summaries of a household's history, a farm coping with crisis, how a conflict was resolved, etc., short, colourful descriptions of situations encountered by the team stories recounted by local people.
14. *Folklore, Songs and Poetry*: They are always in local language using local terminology. They reveal a great deal about values, history, practices, who and what of issues in the community.
15. *Wealth Ranking*: This is a range of methods to identify groups or clusters of household according to relative wealth or well-being. This can easily identify the different economic status of various families in a community.
16. *Transect Walk*: Walking around the community with a specific purpose can bring lot of data. The walking group shall consist of a multidisciplinary team.
17. *Focus Group Discussion*: This is guiding discussion among a group of the community memebrs on a focused theme or issue on the community.
18. *SWOT Analysis*: This seeks to analyse the Strength, Weakness, Opportunities and Threats of a community or group in their specific contexts.
19. *Problem Tree*: It depicts the problems of a community in a shape of a tree. While the roots represent the causes of the problems with consequent causes, the trunk part shows their consequences and their effects in branches.
20. *Local Histories*: It is the detailed accounts of the past, of

how things have changed, particularly focusing on relationships and trends. They may be of technology histories or crop histories.

Apart from these listed methods the different agencies developed and use various methods for their situational purpose.

## Field Applications of PRA

Participatory Rural Appraisal since its inception has been widely applied at various levels of development process. There are interesting examples form organisations at various parts of the world in the field application of PRA and its consequent effects. Adriance (1995), describes the case study of the Siaya Health Education, Water and Sanitation (SHEWAS) project, first implemented in 1990, and focuses particularly on its use of PRA as a means of stimulating community participation in the identification and planning of water and sanitation micro projects. PRA techniques used by the project include mapping, transects, household discussions (instead of interviews and no questionnaires!), timeliness, collection of technical data, institutions analysis, problem ranking and decision-matrices (for selecting water systems technology). Visually oriented and participatory methods, controlled for the most part by the participants themselves.

### *The Use of PRA in Conservation Expeditions*

Pocknell and Annaly (1995), have studied the use of some of the PRA techniques to carry out a survey of land-use patterns and ecology with the indigenous Kuranko people who live adjacent to the reserve. The PRA approach enabled them to gain insights into local ecology, resource use and attitudes that a conventional expedition would not have obtained. They felt that the major value of RRA was in providing a quick yet thorough feel of the main processes occurring, rather than in providing figures to be acted upon. Perhaps most importantly, PRA allowed the needs, attitudes and aspirations of local villagers to be given a voice in the context of future conservation objectives.

Gosselink and Hoeberichts (1996), analyses the use of participatory research when applied to large scale irrigation systems. PRA was considered the most suitable methodology because it provides scope and opportunities for water users to express their perceptions. This approach is different from IIMI-Pakistan's conventional approach to data collection (e.g., primary data collection using questionnaires) because it involves water users as partners rather than sources of information. The need for a different approach was illustrated recently by water users living in a watercourse where IIMI had been collecting data for three years. The villagers revolted against IIMI's presence and would not allow the staff to visit the village or ask any more questions.

***PRA in Art Work***

Gant (2000), conducted a study for New Deal for Communities, a Government Regeneration initiative in Blakenall of Walsall, a town located 6 miles north of Birmingham in the UK. She herself a community art worker applied participatory approaches in the study. The study clearly states that Participatory Appraisal enables people to participate in an open debate, to have their say and actively determine key issues. Community Arts also attempts to give people the tools to be confident participants and then go on to help communities discover, develop and use their creative abilities, through the arts, to express themselves and to find their voice. It is the interplay between the two which enables both workers and participants to see things differently, to think laterally and to come up with new answers and discover new solutions.

Rodríguez (1998) describes the experiences of a Venezuelan NGO, EcoNatura, in carrying out a conflict resolution project and concludes that while PRA has been useful for initiating the communication process between the Park management authority and the local communities, there is a limit to the extent to which PRA can contribute to the resolution of existing conflicts in the Park. The achievements of the application of PRA are the following. A space for organising ideas, bridging a communication gap, development of a positive working relationship between

INPARQUES and the Pemón, and changes in policy-making. The PRA methods used, such as the resource use matrix allowed the Pemón to express their views of the Park, a perspective which focuses on their own valuation of natural resources and puts them in the centre of the park and not outside it.

***PRA in Psychiatry***

Foss and Aune (2000), studies PLA as a tool in participant process orientated evaluation in the field of drug prevention psychiatry in Norway. Participatory approaches have been included in the project to facilitate process oriented, participant evaluation. PLA tools have been used in three phases of the evaluation: evaluation of the pre-project phase, evaluation mid-way and finally by the end of the project period. A participatory approach in this project has been one of many ways of working. They felt that PLA approaches have made a more user-participant analysis and evaluation of the processes possible. Attitudes that are important in participatory work, e.g., listening to and learning from participants, the belief that people can do it themselves, etc., have underpinned each stage of the project. Participatory techniques have been used in processes, to aid us to think, discuss, evaluate and plan together with different participants. The facilitators, as outsiders, have had roles as facilitators in the evaluation not being directly involved in the project work at any time.

**Field Applications of PRA in India**

Kasivelu *et al.* (1995), describe the use of PRA in the rehabilitation of an irrigation tank at a village in Tamil Nadu. The use of participatory methodologies based on open attitudes and behaviour was found to be more effective than the conventional approach based on the collection of statistics collection and the soliciting of farmers' participation. Under the conventional approach, despite the farmer discussions, participation of the local community had still been limited to the extraction of information, for subsequent analysis away from the village. The new approach enabled the farmers and the Agricultural Engineering Department

(AED) personnel to develop an effective working partnership. Collection of data was more rapid and the information obtained was more concise, targeted and relevant to the project. The maps also provided a good basis for planning the subsequent engineering survey, which saved time and money. The use of PRA in the SMIT programme provides a good example of the effectiveness and potential of adopting a more participatory approach in the execution of Government development projects.

Narayanswamy and Borain (2005), conducted a study on the practice of Participatory Rural Appraisal (PRA) among the NGOs in Tamil Nadu, with particular focus on an efficiency of participatory methods. It has found that PRA has emerged as an effective approach and method to empower people especially the poor, the weak and the deprived. Rural development being redefined as participatory development, stresses on people taking the leading role in the process and programmes of development. It highlights the practice of PRA among the NGOs, comparative assessment of survey and PRA and the overall performance of PRA in the rural sector. The study finds out that the participatory approaches empower the people, particularly women and the marginalized in areas of gathering and analyzing information, in decision-making and in implementation and evaluating projects. The study used various methods like reliability, timeliness, rapidity, accuracy, cost effectiveness, adequacy, etc., to assess the efficacy of the PRA methods.

There has been some micro level research done in Kerala on the efficacy of participatory tools and participation in the local level development. Panchayat Level Participatory Resource Mapping (PRM) developed by the Centre for Earth Science Studies (CESS) in collaboration with the State Land Use Board and KSSP in the early 1990s has emerged as an important component of the Panchayat level planning in the State.

Srikumar (2000), attempted to make an assessment of the Participatory Resource Management (PRM) at the Panchayat, district and State levels. The principal findings of the study are the following: (i) PRM have given confidence to people to participate in scientific and technical activities and the information generated by them is found to be useful, (ii) This is a big step towards empowerment. Literacy empowers the individual but resource mapping empowers the society, (iii) However, as technical skills are involved, adequate preparatory work on the part of the Panchayati is essential, (iv) A technical support group, preferably in the vicinity of Krishi Bhavan, needs to be formed to conduct not only PRM but the planning exercise as well, (v) PRM data are not adequate for total plan preparation; a comprehensive data bank may be developed at the Panchayat level, (vi) Voluntary agencies should help the process at the initial stages; but over the time, their role should become progressively small, and (vii) Development programmes may be worked out on the basis of micro watershed. The study has clearly brought out significance of a participatory tool like participatory resource mapping and moreover the need of a voluntary organization in applying such tool.

The feasibility and effectiveness of participatory approach, methods, and tools in the decentralized development process of the Panchayati Raj Institutions (PRIs) is the focus of the study by Joseph (2000), in Nenmeni Grama Panchayat of Wayanad district, the area of this research. They found that: (i) The participatory approach facilitates the evolution of sustainable people's structures and systems at the Grama Sabha and Panchayat levels, which enable local population to become creative partners of the development process, (ii) It makes the target population capable of adopting and using appropriate participatory methods and tools in a systematic and scientific manner throughout the development process, (iii) It facilitates the evolution and application of participatory methods and tools which are specific to each component of the development process, and (iv) It ensures people's participation at a higher level of intensity in the ongoing Panchayati level learning, planning, and action process thereby designing people-centred action plans and projects for the Panchayat. The list of tools used includes: (i) social and resource mapping; (ii) seasonality analysis; (iii) time line; (iv) farm profile; (v) inflow and outflow analysis; (vi) socio-economic dimension ranking; (vii) transect walk, and (viii) watershed maps.

B. Ramesh (2000), in his project located at Kalady Grama Panchayat in Ernakulam district, has attempted to utilise participatory research methods for data collection. The project has completed resource mapping, socio-economic analysis and sector specific studies and on that basis a draft master plan for the Panchayat has been prepared. Attempts have also been made to develop low cost techniques for the large scale application of tissue culture in ornamental and medicinal plants and technological upgradation of handicrafts.

The participatory tools including PRA has received wide acceptance in research dimensions and in achieving participation in the development. The NGOs have used PRA in a range of programmes from care of psychiatric patients to art conservation. In all of them, the practitioners have found the tools of PRA in ensuring peoples ownership than any other methodology of social development. As PRA offers an insider's autonomy, the practitioners develop new tools and practices in the application of PRA. The challenges and limitation of application of PRA invites for a critical appraisal of PRA and its ramifications.

# 5

# Profile of NGOs and Beneficiaries

The NGOs in India have received applause for the good they have done as well as criticism for what they exist and function. A realistic appraisal on nature of NGOs, their philosophy, infrastructure and similar details can give a truthful picture of them. Similarly, an analysis of the profile of the beneficiaries of NGOs would provide a clear understanding of the population they cater to.

## Profile of the NGOs

The study covered eight NGOs which have practiced participatory approaches in the organisations and one organisation, promoted by Department of Forests, Government of Kerala (which could be called as GONGO, Government Owned NGO). The organisations were Arsha Bharath, Meppadi, Brahmagiri Development Society (BDS), Meenanagadi, Joint Voluntary Action for Legal Alternative (JVALA), Kalpetta, Rural Agency for Social and Technological Advancement (RASTA), Kambalackad, Shreyas, Sulthan Battery, Voluntary Organisation for Innovative and Collective Education (VOICE), Sulthan Battery, Wayanad Social Service Society (WSSS), Mananthavady, Women Welfare Association (WWA), Vaduvamchal and North Wayanad Forest Development Agency (NWFDA), Mananthavady.

***Arshabharath***

Arshabharath meaning 'the India of the Sages' was founded in1987 by a team of socially enlightened youth of Wayanad, as a civil society response to the deteriorating situation in Wayanad. It has the mission of nurturing holistic life styles and promoting sustainable development solutions, particularly among farmers, women and youth. They focus mainly on the home district of Wayanad and have active presence in 14 Grama Panchayats of six development Blocks. The activities in the home district include SHGs for women and men, watershed programmes, rural development, tribal development, health promotion and nature conservation. The same programmes are done at Nilgiri district in Tamil Nadu. The organisation's involvement in Idukki district of Kerala is through PSH (Partnership in Sexual Health) projects for HIV/AIDS prevention and intervention among target groups supported by the State government.

***Brahmagiri Development Society (BDS)***

BDS was established in 1996 with the main objective of dairy development in Wayanad. This was an effort initiated by the dairy Development Department of the State government along with leaders in cooperative sector. The main target area of BDS is Wayanad district, where they have value added services for dairy development and does watershed projects. BDS gives consultancy service for dairy promotion in all the districts of the State. The organisation was formed after extensive PRA and they follow participatory approaches in their programmes.

***Joint Voluntary Action for Legal Alternative (JVALA)***

JVALA which began service in 1998 was the effort of the experienced social workers in Wayanad for social development on a right based approach. The organisation focuses on the home district of Wayanad. They do rural development, women empowerment, tribal development and child development programmes. JVALA runs the child line programme in Wayanad.

It has active presence in 25 Gram Panchayats of three development Block of the district. They have applied participatory approaches in their programmes.

***Rural Agency for Soil and Technological Advancement (RASTA)***

RASTA strives to impart development oriented education with the intention of improving the socio-economic conditions of the needy. It promotes conservation, imparts environmental education, and disseminates eco-friendly rural technologies, besides conducting research in sustainable agriculture. Its Director T.K. Omana was among the 92 women from India nominated for the Nobel Peace Prize for 2005. She started this NGO along with her husband in 1984 after her social work experience from Social Work and Research Centre (SWRC) at Tilonia in Rajasthan. They have implemented number of projects aimed at empowerment of backward communities. RASTA, a secular NGO, was a pioneer in introducing participatory approaches in the district. Their main area of operation is Wayanad while they had rural development programmes in Kasaragode district and government sponsored community based drinking water supply project (*Jalanidhi*) at Calicut district. They have active presence in 26 Grama Panchayats of eight development Blocks.

***Shreyas***

Shreyas is the official social development organization of the Malankara Catholic Diocese of Bathery to uplift the poor and marginalized and was started in 1979. It is one of the leading NGOs working in south India for the development of marginal farmers, tribal, women, children and senior citizens and the largest one among the NGOs under study. They involve in agriculture development, tribal development, women empowerment, micro credit, children's club, youth clubs, housing, sanitation and micro enterprises. The programme area of Shreyas spread over 15 civil districts of Kerala, Tamil Nadu and Karnataka and covers 28 Blocks and 99 Grama Panchayats. Shreyas has initiated participatory approaches in the district and had applied PRA massively in its field programmes and organisational management. They have given training on PRA to other NGOs and developed new tools in participatory approaches.

### *Voluntary Organisation for Innovative and Collective Education (VOICE)*

VOICE was started in 1996 with the objective of promoting development of the tribal and women and agriculture sector of the district. It has active presence through CBOs in 25 Gram Panchayats of three development Blocks. Their activities include regeneration of indigenous farming practices, protection of traditional food habits of tribal people, promotion of agriculture, women empowerment programmes and development of small enterprises. Although VOICE focuses on the home district, their women empowerment programmes are spread in the northern districts of the State. They have applied participatory approaches in their programmes.

### *Wayanad Social Service Society (WSSS)*

WSSS is committed to see the social realities from the perspective of the poor and the marginalized whose strives, dreams and aspirations we share. It was established in 1974 for the development of agriculture and animal husbandry, community health, co-operative credit unions, women's development, skills development, housing and sanitation. WSSS is the official social service organ of the catholic diocese of Manathavady. They have active presence in 41 Grama Panchayats of seven development Blocks, mainly in the home district and in Nilgiri and Kannur district. Their presence in Malappuram district is through community managed drinking water supply (*Jalanidhi*) projects. WSSS was a pioneer in introducing participatory approaches in the district and trained a lot of agencies and personnel on PRA.

### *Women's Welfare Association (WWA)*

Women's Welfare Association has been serving rural poor in the

Wayanad district since 1978. It promotes integrated people centred rural development for improving the quality of life and the living conditions of village communities irrespective of caste, creed and political leaning. The management of WWA is by Catholic Church and its congregations. Women from different walks of life are members of its General Body. They have regular programmes for women empowerment through SHGs, agriculture development, watershed programmes and programmes for tribal development. Their activities are spread mainly in Wayanad district and partly in Nilgiri district. They cover three development Blocks with active presence in 10 Gram Panchayats. They have followed participatory practices in their programmes.

***North Wayanad Forest Development Authority (NWFDA)***

This is initiated by the forest department of State government. NWFDA is a registered body consisting of the member Vanam Samrakshana Samities (VSS). VSS is the local association of the people living in the fringe area of the forest. NWFDA began in 2002 as the result of the Participatory Forest Management Programme (PFM). PFM facilitates conservation of the forest area with the people living in near the forest. While the VSS is managed by the committee of the local people and its secretary is an official of the forest department. Government provides fund to VSS for the conservation activities. The micro plan for conservation of the forest by every VSS is done through extensive PRA in that area.

*Legal Entity of the Organisation*

All the organisations studied are registered societies under the Indian Societies Registrations Act. They have a general body and an executive body guiding the activities of the organisations. The North Wayanad Forest Development Authority is also registered under the societies registration act with government officials and leaders of people's groups. They work for forest conservation and allied activities. It functions according to the by law of the agency with government guidelines.

*Type of Building of NGO*

Six organisations operate from their own building. Out of the eight NGOs three (Shreyas, WSSS, WWA) are sponsored by the church. They are large in size and have own land and buildings. RASTA and Arshabharath are secular in nature and established with own land and buildings. The other three secular ones, Jwala, Voice and BDS are comparatively small in size and they operate from rented building. NWFDA operates from the divisional office of the forest department of the State government.

*Geographical Area of Operation of the Agencies*

All the organisations concentrate their activities in home district of Wayanad. The church based NGOs (Shreyas, WSSS and WWA) have regular programmes in certain districts of Tamil Nadu and Karnataka in the nearby southern States. They operate mainly around the churches in those areas. The presence of RASTA and Arshabharath in other districts of Kerala is through certain time bound projects like the Jalanidhi

**Table 5.1:** Area of operation of NGOs

| *Name of organisation* | *States covered* | *Districts covered* | *No. of Development Blocks covered* | *No. of Gram Panchayats covered* |
|---|---|---|---|---|
| **Arsha Bharath** | Kerala, Tamil Nadu | Wayanad, Nilgiri, Idukki | 6 | 14 |
| **BDS** | Kerala | All districts of Kerala | | |
| **JVALA** | Kerala | Wayanad | 3 | 25 |
| **RASTA** | Kerala | Wayanad, Calicut, Kasaragode | 8 | 26 |
| **Shreyas** | Kerala, Tamil Nadu, Karnataka | Malappuram, Calicut, Wayanad, Kasaragode, Dakshina Kannada, Shimoga, Nilgiris Chikmagalore, Uduppi | 28 | 99 |
| **VOICE** | Kerala | Wayanad | 3 | 25 |
| **WSSS** | Kerala, Tamil Nadu | Wayanad, Nilgiri, Kannur, Malappuram | 7 | 41 |
| **WWA** | Kerala, Tamil Nadu | Wayanad, Nilgiri | 3 | 10 |
| **NWFDA** | Kerala | Wayanad | 1 | 9 |

(Community managed drinking water supply project, implemented by Government of Kerala with the aid of the World Bank) and HIV/AIDS prevention projects. WSSS and RASTA too had taken up Jalanidhi projects in other districts not represented by their regular programmes. They do not have regular programmes in those districts. The grassroot level programmes of BDS are limited to the Wayanad district while they give consultancy service to certain programmes outside the district. NWFDA functions in the specified areas of the North Wayanad divisional office of the Forest Department, while there is another FDA in part of the district for the same purposes. The important activities of VOICE are in Wayanad district while their women groups' activities are spread through other five Northern districts of Kerala. Jvala's activities are limited to Wayanad alone.

Shreays, the largest among the studied organisation have the largest area of operation, followed by WSSS and RASTA. While the organisations were established for intervention in Wayanad district, they have branched out to other districts for the implementation of specific projects. This has given them statewide presence and improved their capacity in all dimensions. Nevertheless they remain focused on Wayanad.

### *Details of Staff in the Organisations*

All the organisations have paid staff and voluntary staff supporting their field level activities. Voluntary staffs operate at the grassroot

**Table 5.2:** Staff strength of the organisations

| *Name of organisation* | *Total paid staff* | *Voluntary staff* | *Total staff* | *Office staff* | *Field staff* |
|---|---|---|---|---|---|
| Arsha Bharath | 23 | 8 | 31 | 17 | 14 |
| BDS | 21 | 0 | 21 | 8 | 13 |
| Jwala | 15 | 3 | 18 | 0 | 0 |
| RASTA | 12 | 13 | 25 | 4 | 8 |
| Shreyas | 240 | 900 | 1140 | 22 | 218 |
| VOICE | 21 | 0 | 21 | 7 | 14 |
| WSSS | 45 | 252 | 45 | 28 | 17 |
| WWA | 34 | 62 | 96 | 5 | 29 |
| NWFDA | Only one paid staff. The forest department officials share the responsibilities. The CBO leaders do voluntary service | | | | |

level as the leaders of Self-Help Groups (SHGs), SGH federations at the Gram Panchayat level and leaders of various committees in different projects. The large volume of voluntary staff, much higher than the paid staff, depicts the people's support and resource mobilisation capacity of the organisations. The number of staff is in proportion to the size of the organisations, i.e., the large organisation like Shreyas has highest number of staff. NWFDA has appointed one staff from the organisation to facilitate the field level operations of the FDA, while all other activities are done by the forest department officials assigned for the work, and by peoples leaders grassroot level forest conservation committees known as Vanam Samrakshana Samity (VSS) in the fringe areas and Eco Development Committees (EDC) in the wildlife areas.

**Table 5.3:** Classification of paid staff according to qualification

| *Name of organization* | *Below graduation* | *Graduation* | *MSW* | *PG and above* | *Technically qualified* |
|---|---|---|---|---|---|
| Arsha Bharath | 5 | 8 | 7 | 3 | 2 |
| BDS | 13 | 1 | — | 2 | 5 |
| Jwala | 7 | 8 | — | 3 | — |
| RASTA | 15 | 7 | — | 3 | 3 |
| Shreyas | 182 | 28 | 8 | 14 | 8 |
| VOICE | 14 | 4 | 2 | 1 | — |
| WSSS | 2 | 24 | 2 | 15 | 5 |
| WWA | 12 | 12 | 3 | 7 | — |
| NWFDA | 1 | — | — | — | — |

The education qualifications of the paid staff of the organisations indicate the professional capacity of the organisations. The NGOs mostly employ graduates and those studied below graduation. They receive training and guided experience from the organisations. Five organisations have professionally qualified social workers (MSW) who are appointed for specific projects and in specific positions like counsellors and project managers. Five organisations have technically qualified staff like engineers and agronomist appointed for specific projects like watershed. The low salary scale of NGOs fails to attract qualified professionals. The quality of the staff influences the functioning and professionalism of the organisations.

**Table 5.4:** Classification of Staff according to their Experience

| *Name of organization* | *Below 1 year* | *2 years* | *3 years* | *4 years* | *5-10 years* | *Above 10 years* |
|---|---|---|---|---|---|---|
| Arsha Bharath | — | — | — | — | — | 23 |
| BDS | 2 | 2 | 3 | 3 | 11 | — |
| Jwala | — | | 3 | 6 | 5 | 4 |
| RASTA | — | 1 | — | — | 12 | 12 |
| Shreyas | 35 | 22 | 40 | 38 | 73 | 32 |
| VOICE | — | 8 | 2 | 1 | 7 | 3 |
| WSSS | 2 | 14 | 4 | 5 | 9 | 11 |
| WWA | 12 | 2 | 1 | 1 | 18 | 14 |
| NWFDA | 1 | — | — | — | — | — |

If the educational qualification of the staff is an indicator of professionalism, the years of experience in the organisation is an indicator of the dedication and commitment of the staff to the organisation. Very interestingly more than half of the staff in all the NGOs is with them for more than five years. The strength of some organisations is the staff working with them for more than ten years, some of them even from the beginning of the organisation itself. BDS appointed staff for less than last ten years. The long years of service to NGOs demonstrate the dedicated service minded approach of the NGO staff *vis-à-vis* the care for its employees by the NGOs. But there is frequent changes in the professionally qualified personnel; the less educated and trained by the organisation stay for longer period.

### *Target Population of the Organisations*

The Table 5.5 shows the target groups of the NGOs. While the entire organisations serve women and have their own women's groups, only one organisation each (Shreyas and WSSS) have some programmes for the aged and the orphans. Wayanad has a large concentration of tribal communities and eight organisations serve them. Most of them have programmes for children and farmers. But the youth focused programmes are done only by five organisations as also for the scheduled caste communities. Six NGOs network with Panchayati Raj Institutions (PRIs) in their programmes. The response of the beneficiaries corroborates the opinions of the NGO. The beneficiaries may not have complete

**Table 5.5:** Target population of NGOs

| *Target group* | *Response of NGOs* | | *Response of beneficiaries* | |
|---|---|---|---|---|
| | *Frequency* | *Percent* | *Frequency* | *Percent* |
| Women | 9 | 100 | 46 | 51.1 |
| Children | 8 | 88.9 | 41 | 45.6 |
| Aged | 1 | 11.1 | 22 | 24.4 |
| Youth | 5 | 55.6 | 25 | 27.8 |
| Scheduled Tribes | 8 | 88.9 | 39 | 43.3 |
| Scheduled Castes | 5 | 55.6 | 23 | 25.6 |
| Farmers | 8 | 88.9 | 40 | 44.4 |
| Orphans | 1 | 11.1 | 14 | 15.6 |
| Panchayati Raj Institutions | 6 | 66.7 | 13 | 14.4 |

idea of the activities of the NGO. They would be familiar with programmes they come across and the one they have heard of. Nevertheless, the beneficiaries too provide the similar picture on the target population of the NGOs. Beneficiaries identify the priority sectors of the NGOs as women, farmers, children and scheduled tribes. The orphans and the aged are the least target populations of NGOs. The focused groups discussion done with the staff of the NGOs also revealed the priority target groups of the organisations.

The NGOs have put women at the centre of development. It is observed that the social service agenda is limited for these organisations and they do not have much programmes for the orphans and destitutes. The target populations of the NGOs represent the general profile of the kind of service of NGOs in Kerala as well as in the country. While the main scheme of NWFDA is forest protection, they have various social development programmes which were implemented through it.

*Community Based Organisations (CBOs) of the NGOs*

The strength of the NGOs lies in the grassroot level organisation of people. The NGOs organize different types of CBOs as a collective identity and a means for self-help. The largest number of peoples groups is SHGs of women, followed by SHGs of men. The parent organisations form the grassroot level SHGs under federations. Seven NGOs have federations of women SHGs while four have federations of men SHGs. Eight NGOs have groups of

**Table 5.6:** Details of Community Based Organisations of NGOs

| *Organisations* | *Self Help Groups (SHGs)* | | *Federations SHGs* | | *Children's Groups* | *Groups of the Aged* | *Farmers' Groups* | *Others* | *Total CBOs* |
|---|---|---|---|---|---|---|---|---|---|
| | *Women* | *Men* | *Women SHGs* | *Men SHGs* | | | | | |
| Arsha Bharath | 105 | 100 | 1 | 4 | 1 | — | — | 1 | 212 |
| BDS | — | — | — | — | — | — | 192 | — | 192 |
| Jwala | 100 | — | 5 | — | 28 | — | — | 1 | 134 |
| RASTA | 437 | 18 | 1 | — | 4 | — | 15 | — | 475 |
| Shreyas | 1722 | 423 | 56 | 51 | 461 | 67 | 65 | 261 | 3106 |
| VOICE | 110 | 10 | 1 | — | 20 | — | 1 | 1 | 143 |
| WWA | 840 | 110 | 4 | 4 | 60 | — | — | — | 1018 |
| WSSS | 655 | 108 | 65 | 65 | 20 | — | 85 | 35 | 1033 |
| NWFDA | 30 | 10 | — | — | 9 | — | — | 18 | 67 |

children and five have groups for aged. The NWFDA has Vanam Sanrakshana Samity (VSS) which serves the purpose of the forest protection, the prime agenda of the FDA. The other groups are supportive to this purpose. BDS have only farmers groups formed with the aim of promotion of dairying. In the number of CBOs, Shreyas has the highest number of CBOs followed by WSSS and WWA. The number and performance of CBOs is an indication of the range of activities and the grassroot level participation in the NGO activities.

*Fields of Activities of the Organisation*

The NGOs involve in a variety of activities as per the mission of the organisations as well as by the need of beneficiaries of the NGOs. All of them have programmes for financial advancement through different income generation programmes, including micro enterprises by six organisations. Most of them involve in health care, educational upliftment, agriculture development, watershed, women empowerment, livestock development, sanitation, environment conservation and legal literacy programmes. All of them have some type of community based organisation in the form of SHGs and their federations, farmers groups, children's groups and youth clubs. The hardware components of housing, sanitary latrines and drinking water projects are done by half of

**Table 5.7:** The fields of activities of the organisations

| *Fields of activities* | *Response of organisations* | | *Response of beneficiaries* | |
|---|---|---|---|---|
| | *Frequency* | *Percent* | *Frequency* | *Percent* |
| Agriculture | 8 | 88.9 | 72 | 80.0 |
| Health | 7 | 77.8 | 61 | 67.8 |
| Education | 7 | 77.8 | 58 | 64.4 |
| Income generation programmes | 9 | 100.0 | 72 | 80.0 |
| Community Based organizations | 7 | 77.8 | 52 | 57.8 |
| Watershed | 7 | 77.8 | 47 | 52.2 |
| Drinking water | 6 | 66.7 | 39 | 43.3 |
| Sanitation | 6 | 66.7 | 48 | 53.3 |
| Livestock development | 7 | 77.8 | 50 | 55.6 |
| Women empowerment | 8 | 88.9 | 67 | 74.4 |
| Child development | 7 | 77.8 | 49 | 54.4 |
| Human rights | 4 | 44.4 | 27 | 30.0 |
| Housing | 5 | 55.6 | 42 | 46.7 |
| Institution building | 4 | 44.4 | 29 | 32.2 |
| Environment Conservation | 8 | 88.9 | 53 | 58.9 |
| Micro Enterprises | 6 | 66.7 | 52 | 57.8 |
| Legal literacy | 8 | 88.9 | 42 | 46.7 |
| Micro Finance | 3 | 33.3 | 10 | 11.1 |
| Insurance | 2 | 22.2 | 25 | 27.8 |
| Others | 8 | 88.9 | 3 | 3.3 |

the organisations. Micro finance and micro insurance are done by three and two agencies respectively. But the SHGs do the service of micro financing through their thrift and credits. Moreover, the NGOs provide them money for credit among its members by linking the SHGs to the banks. The NGO sector has entered into many new areas of operation with innovative strategies following participatory approaches. Many such initiatives like participatory micro enterprises can play an important role in accelerating the development process of the developing nations like India (Anna, 1995; Raja, 2000; Ravindran, 1997). The NGOs in general cover all the social development areas of Wayanad.

The NGOs find the funds for their programmes from multiple sources. All the organisations depend mainly on government sponsored projects for funding. The main government projects aided by various departments of State and Central governments are in watershed, micro enterprises, agricultural development, drinking water supply (Jalanidhi), HIV/AIDS prevention,

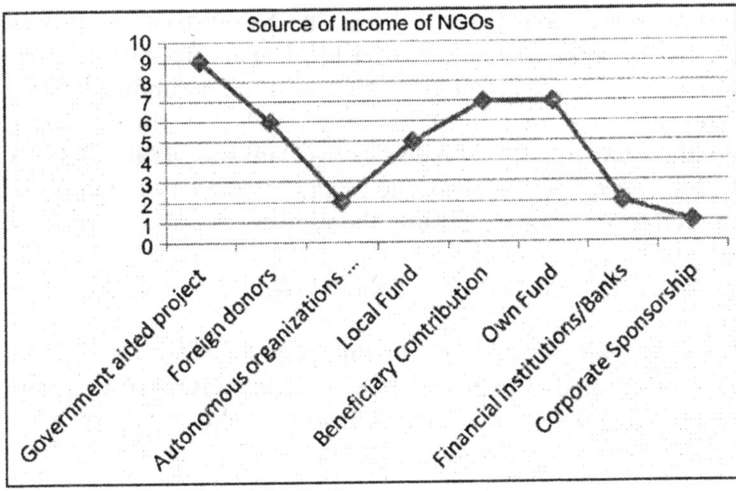


**Fig. 5.1:** Sources of fund for NGOs
Source of Income of NGOs

sanitation and housing. The utilisation of government aid challenges the common notion of foreign funding of NGOs. The paradigm shift in the government policy (Millennium Development Goals No. 8, public private partnership in development) has triggered the partnership with third sector in social development.

Except BDS, Voice and NWFDA all other NGOs have received foreign aid for various projects. But the flow of foreign fund has declined stating that Kerala is a developed State. Seven organisations have own fund mobilised through previous projects and local sources. Most of the organisations mobilise beneficiaries' share in implementation of the programmes. Five organisations collect funds from local sources like the Panchayati Raj Institutions; while two have endeavoured network with banks for fund mobilisation; and only one NGO ventured for corporate sources—an area yet to be tapped well. Two have support from autonomous institutions like Government research institutes.

The financial security of the NGOs is challenging. The foreign funding to NGOs in Kerala is fast depleting as many donors have moved out of the State, said the organisations' head and staff in the FGDs. The aid of the government agencies may vary depending on government policies. The NGOs have not proven efficient in mobilising funds from local and corporate sources. While assessing the problems of NGOs in India, funding has not been much an issue but the localism, small size, fragmentation and the failure to institutionalise them (Dantwala, 1998). But lack of fund, *inter alia*, has been one of the important limitations of the NGOs for institutionalising themselves.

## Profile of the Beneficiaries of the NGO

The study used an interview schedule with ten beneficiaries, who have participated in PRA activities, in nine NGOs for the study; thus totalling ninety respondents from the field. This part of the study deals with the demographic profile of the respondents.

### *Gender of Beneficiaries*

Out of the total 90 respondents 42.2 per cent (38) are men and 57.8 per cent (52) are women. Women outweigh men in the target group of the NGOs. In proportion to that the respondents too have more women than men. Women members participate in large numbers in the activities of the NGOs, including the PRA exercises.

### *Age of Beneficiaries*

The most active young period was spared for NGO activities. Forty-four per cent of respondents were in the age-group of 30 to 40. Two-third of the respondents were in the age-group of thirty to fifty. This analysis shows that the people associate with NGO activities in their active age-group (*see* Fig. 5.2).

### *Marital Status of Beneficiaries*

Eighty-nine per cent of respondents (80 persons) were married. 6.7 per cent (6 persons) respondents were unmarried and 4.4 per cent (4 persons) widows too attended participatory activities of NGO. The participation of either the husband or of wife is the indication of the family for involving in the NGO activities.

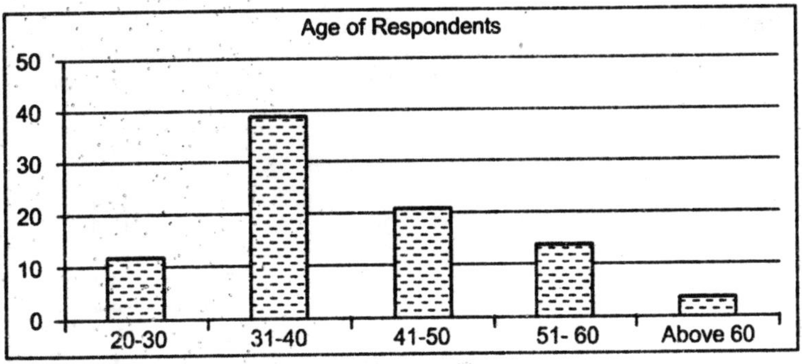


**Fig. 5.2:** Age-wise classification of respondents

*Religion of the Beneficiaries*

The religion-wise distribution of the respondents is in proportion with the religious distribution of district as well. The Hindus and Christians, who constitute the largest population in the district, constitute about forty-eight per cent each of respondents. The Hindus constitute 47.8 and the Christians 48.9 per cent. The Muslims are only 3.3 per cent. The social involvement of Muslim especially women among them is restricted by the religion. The NGOs, irrespective of their religious affinity, caters to people of all religions in their service.

*Family-Size of the Beneficiaries*

Nearly one-third of the respondents are from nuclear families, with three or less members in their families. Sixty-two per cent of the respondents are from families which have four to six members which mean father, mother and two or three children or grand-parents. There is one respondent who lives alone, while another two have nine and ten members in their families. Five respondent families have only two members at home. The family size of the respondents depicts the cross-section of the family in the district with average four or five members per house.

*Education of the Beneficiaries*

The NGO activists focus on the lower strata of the society, who are often less educated and poor. The study confirms this fact.

**Table 5.8:** Family-size of the respondents

| Number of family members | Frequency | Percentage |
|---|---|---|
| 1 | 1 | 1.1 |
| 2 | 5 | 5.6 |
| 3 | 22 | 24.4 |
| 4 | 36 | 40.0 |
| 5 | 16 | 17.8 |
| 6 | 4 | 4.4 |
| 7 | 4 | 4.4 |
| 8 | 0 | 0 |
| 9 | 1 | 1.1 |
| 10 | 1 | 1.1 |
| Total | 90 | 100.0 |

Just above one-third of the respondents (34.4%) have primary education. 36.7 per cent (33 respondents) have high school education. It shows that seventy-one per cent of the respondents have only school education. However, 22.2 per cent of respondents have studied up to higher secondary. There are only six respondents (6.6%) with degree or above education. This fact explores that the educated do not usually attend the NGO activities. The illiterate and those with basic education dominate among the participants in the Gram Sabha meetings of the Panchayati Raj system in Kerala (Muraleedharan, 2006). The actual participation in development programmes, both in the government and non-government sector is by illiterates and less educated.

## *Family Income of the Beneficiaries*

The monthly family income of the respondents reveals the financial profile of the NGOs beneficiaries. The target group of the NGOs is the economically backward communities. Fifty-four per cent of the respondents have only income less than Rs. 2000 per month; thirteen per cent of respondents each fall in the income category of Rs. 2001–3000 and in 3001–4000. There are only three families with monthly income above Rs. 5,000. The findings on monthly family income are not absolute as there are chances that people state their income less than the actual one. Eventhough it

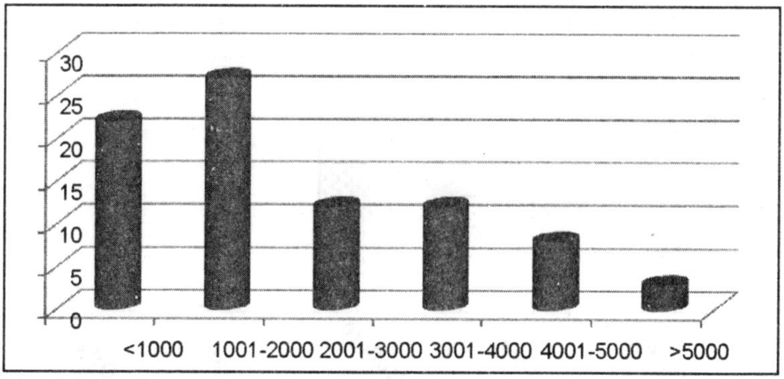


**Fig. 5.3:** Monthly family income of respondents

is observed that the respondents are far behind the general stream of the society in their financial capacity. The participation of people in the Gram Sabha of the Panchayati Raj system in the country too has similar profile (Muraleedharan, 2006). The participants in the development programmes, both in the government and non-government sector are from financially backward classes.

### *Family Status of the Beneficiaries*

Agriculture is the backbone of the district of Wayanad. Agriculturists and farmers are an important target group of the NGOs. Two-thirds of the respondents are from agriculture based families. The other largest category is of still poorer group of daily wage workers, consisting of twenty-seven per cent. The agriculturists and daily wage earners comprise ninety per cent of the respondents and they represent the backward sections of the society. There are 3.3 per cent people involved in small scale business and one respondent is professionally employed. The families of about 6 per cent (5 respondents) have other different backgrounds like self-employment or returned from job abroad. Obviously, the respondents hail from poor family background.

### *Duration of Association of the Beneficiaries with the NGO*

The largest number of respondents, a quarter of them, is associated with the respective NGOs for more than ten years. More than

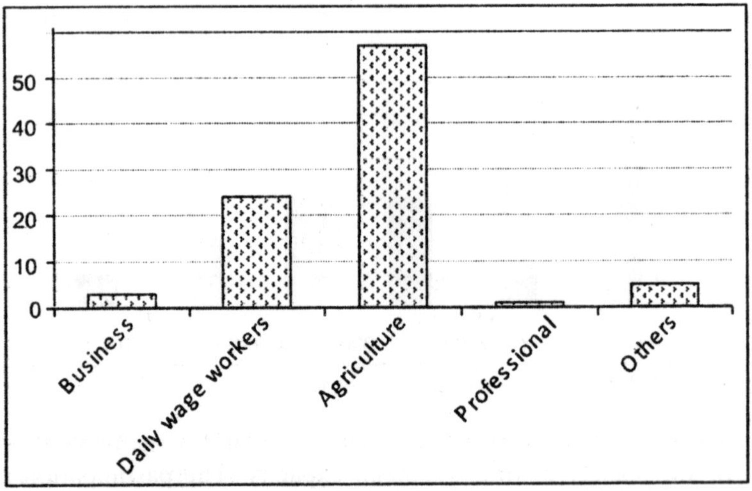


**Fig. 5.4:** Family status of respondents

half of the respondents involved with the NGOs for more than five years. Twenty-three per cent have been to the NGO activities for less than three years, so as another thirty-three per cent for three to five years. The tenure of interaction is decided by the entry of the NGO to their respective communities. For most of the respondents, they maintain their active relation with the NGOs since their first contact with it. The relationship of the NGOs with the beneficiaries is mutually caring and hence they cherish their relationship. The staff of the NGOs plays a crucial role in maintaining relation with the beneficiaries. This shows the capacity of the organisation in maintaining good relation with the staff and beneficiary groups.

**Table 5.9:** Period of association of Beneficiaries with the organization

| *Period of association (in years)* | *Frequency* | *Percent* |
|---|---|---|
| 1-3 | 21 | 23.3 |
| 4-5 | 21 | 23.3 |
| 6-7 | 9 | 10.0 |
| 8-10 | 17 | 18.9 |
| >10 | 22 | 24.4 |
| Total | 90 | 100 |

### *Position of Beneficiaries in the Community Based Organisation* **(CBO)**

The respondents are active leaders at their community based organisations like SHGs, (Self-Help Groups) watershed committees and VSS (Vanam Samrakshana Samity). Two-third of them have been either president or secretary of the CBO, the two powerful and responsible positions in the CBO. About 7.7 per cent (even respondents) have handled finance of the CBO as the treasurer while 12.2 per cent had been executive committee members. There were 22.2 per cent (twenty respondents) who had been on other leadership roles like member of monitoring committee in the VSS or member of advisory committee. Some of the respondents have held more than one position in different terms. About eleven per cent respondents have not held any position in the CBOs.

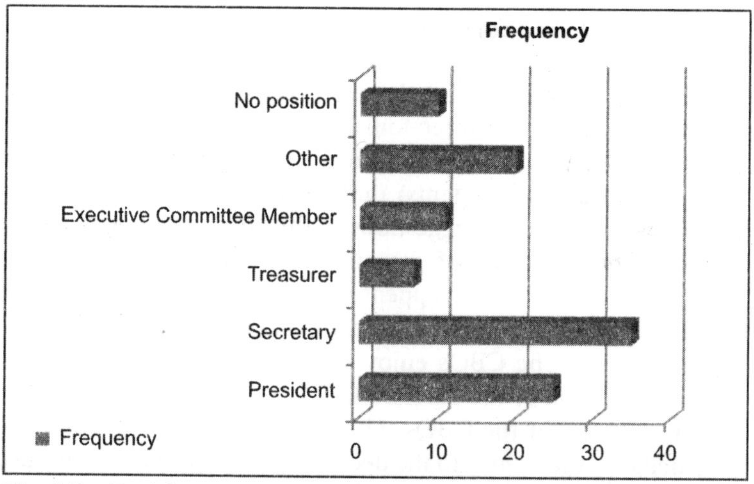


**Fig. 5.5:** Position held by Respondents in the Community Based Organisation (%)

### *Present Position held by the Beneficiaries*

About seventy per cent of respondents are presently involved in the leadership of the CBOs. Ten per cent of them are presidents

**Table 5.10:** Present position of respondents in the CBO

| *Present Position in CBO* | *Frequency* | *Percentage* |
|---|---|---|
| President | 9 | 10.0 |
| Secretary | 10 | 11.1 |
| Treasurer | 1 | 1.1 |
| Executive Committee Member | 12 | 13.3 |
| Other | 32 | 35.6 |
| No position | 26 | 28.9 |
| Total | 90 | 100 |

of their CBOs, while eleven per cent are secretaries. There is one treasurer and 13.3 per cent working as executive committee members. Thirty-six per cent work in other positions like the members of monitoring committees, representatives in SHG federations and members of advisory committees. Twenty-nine per cent do not hold any positions presently.

## Decision-making Process in the CBOs

The beneficiaries opine that the decisions of their CBO are taken by themselves. While three-fourth of respondents (75.6%) said that they take the decision in their general body, twenty-nine per cent opined (26 respondents) that the executive body takes the decisions based on the suggestions of the NGO. Four respondents answered both options of the questions, which means that the decision-making process happens in both ways. The questionnaire had the option that the NGO takes the decision for CBO, which nobody chose. The CBOs enjoy autonomy in their functioning. The involvement of the parent NGO is restricted in the decision-making process of the CBOs. The staff of the organisations also revealed that their entry to the decision-making of CBO is limited to giving suggestions. The people's groups are empowered to take decision of their own for their growth. The internal democracy of the CBO is strong and participatory in nature. Involvement of the community in the decisions which concern their future is a prerequisite in the management of local resources and community development (Bhattacharya, 2001). The CBOs has received adequate autonomy to decide their own destiny.

## Participation of Stakeholders in the CBOs and in the NGOs

The CBOs incorporates the participation of various other organisations and individuals who could contribute to the development efforts of the CBO. The staff of the sponsoring NGO often attends in the meetings and programmes of the CBO as opined by 77 per cent of the respondents. The heads of NGOs too attend the programmes, but not so often as of the staff. The representatives and the members of the CBOs too actively involve in the programmes of the CBO. The local political parties too show interest in the programmes of the CBO so as the representatives of the local clubs. Even though the members of the local self-government have an active role in the programmes of the CBO, their participation in the activities of the CBO is less. The research mostly covered the CBOs established for the watershed programmes. In watershed as well as in some other specific projects a local committee consisting of the representatives of the PRI members, agriculture department, health department, etc. was a proposition in the project itself. It has helped for an inbuilt system of local participation of the local stakeholders in the project activities through the CBO. But the analysis shows that the representatives from the government department and outside agencies scantily participated in the local NGO activities.

**Table 5.11:** Participants in the development programmes of the CBO

| *Participants* | *Frequency* | *Percentage* |
|---|---|---|
| The head of the NGO | 17 | 18.9 |
| Members of the NGO | 69 | 76.7 |
| Representatives of the people's group | 68 | 75.6 |
| Staff of the people's group | 68 | 75.6 |
| Representatives of the local clubs | 13 | 14.4 |
| Representatives of local political parties | 16 | 17.8 |
| Representatives from local health centre | 2 | 2.2 |
| Representatives of PRIs | 4 | 4.4 |
| Others | 2 | 2.2 |

The programmes of the NGO are done in association with other stakeholders. The staff of the agency invariably attends the programmes. The head of the organisation too attend the

**Table 5.12:** Participants in the development programme of the agency

| *Participants* | *Frequency* | *Percentage* |
|---|---|---|
| The head of the NGO | 7 | 77.8 |
| Staff of the NGO | 8 | 88.9 |
| Leaders of the people's group | 7 | 77.8 |
| Members of the people's group | 6 | 66.7 |
| Representatives from local Health Centre | 1 | 11.1 |
| Representatives from Agricultural Department | 5 | 55.6 |
| Representatives of the local clubs | 2 | 22.2 |
| Representatives of local political parties | 3 | 33.3 |
| Representatives of PRIs | 3 | 33.3 |
| Representatives of donor agencies | 6 | 66.7 |
| Others | 1 | 11.1 |

programmes in all the organisations except when the head is holding a higher level government position as in the case of NWFDA. Leaders of the people's groups are also part of the NGO level body and in their programmes. In five NGOs the agriculture department makes active interventions in the agriculture development and watershed projects. The participation of the local clubs, PRI members and political parties are limited in the CBO. But the representatives of the donor agencies are part of the programmes and decision-making process of the NGOs. The donor agencies include the government departments. The important stakeholders in the activities of the government agency are the staff of the agency, beneficiary groups and the local Gram Panchayat.

Bhattacharaya (2001) opines that the NGOs have an important role to play in implementing the village level development programmes. The NGOs need to interface between the State agencies (and other organisations) in the development process. The participation of different State level agencies and similar minded organisations can spur the activities of the CBOs. At the NGO level the programmes are largely attended by the NGO personnel, the sponsored peoples group, the representatives of the line department associating with the project and the donor agencies. The participation of the Government departments is selective that they are project based and not based on the holistic approach. The participation of the local social development institutions especially the PRIs is inadequate. At the grassroot level the CBO members and the NGO personnel are the key players with limited participation of other local agents like PRI. But the FGD with the staff revealed that the PRA workshops held at the CBO level had attracted the participation of members of PRI, members of local clubs and other opinion leaders in the community.

The above discussion unfolded the characteristics of NGOs, the profile of beneficiaries of the NGOs and the decision-making process in the CBOs and the stakeholder participation in the CBO and NGOs. The NGOs involve in many areas which are in need for the public. At the same time they face certain challenges in their existence as well. The beneficiaries of the NGOs—rather partners in the local level development of the community—represent the educationally, financially and socially backward class of the society. While the NGO personnel participate in the regular programmes of the CBOs, the participation of other stakeholders are not significant. The CBOs claims autonomy in decision-making and functioning of their CBO, though they are guided by the sponsoring NGOs.

# 6

# PRA as Applied and Benefited

The NGOs have applied PRA in their various programmes and it fetched benefits, along with its challenges and limitations. This chapter discusses participatory approaches followed by the NGOs in the organisation and application of PRA. Triangulation, an approach followed in PRA is used for analysis. Triangulation means looking at any problem from as many perspectives as possible (FAO, 1994; Norton, 1998). Triangulation tries to ensure that the results of a study are as accurate and unbiased as possible. It is a key tool in establishing trustworthiness of participatory research results. The data is generated from multi-perception analysis of variables from the views of the NGO, the beneficiaries and the staff. The Exhibit 4 shows the sources of triangulation.

The triangulation has happened through the sources of data and at the tools of data collection. While the sources of data were the heads of the NGOs, the staff facilitating participatory practices and the beneficiaries of NGOs, the tools were the questionnaire for heads, focused group discussion for staffs and the interview schedule for beneficiaries. The data collected from multiple sources through multiple tools at similar time are triangulated here. Some variables, which represents the opinion of one group like that of NGO or beneficiaries are presented without triangulation. The chapter sheds light on the rationale for use of participatory practices, stages of the project where PRA has been applied, doing of PRA workshops and trainings, Programmes where PRA is used, peoples participation in participatory programmes, Tools

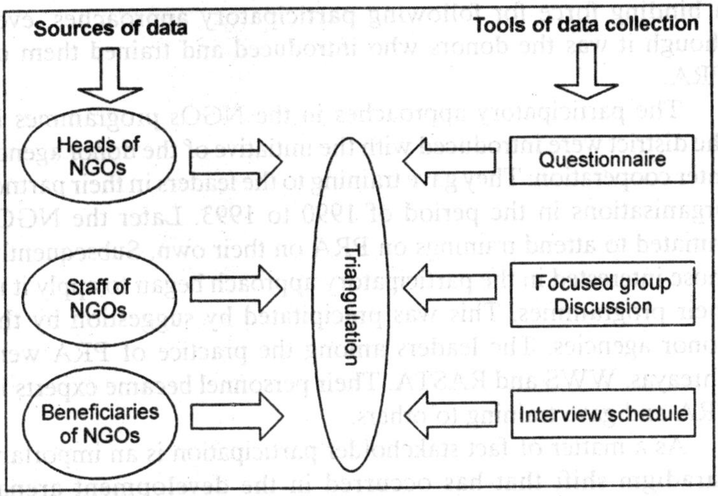


**Exhibit 4 :** Diagrammatic sketch of sources of triangulation

of PRA, Results of Participatory Programmes, Challenges in the application of participatory approaches and Participatory Approaches in Organisations

## Rationale of following Participatory Approaches

The NGOs have adopted stakeholders' participation as a matter of policy in their institution. On the question to why they adopt participatory approaches the NGOs answered that participation has been a policy of the organisations. They adopt PRA also by realising the potential and value of its use. The increased support from the people and staff on the effect of participatory approaches have also helped in following the participatory practices. According to the NGOs the pressure of the donor agencies is not

**Table 6.1:** Reasons for adopting participatory approaches

| *Reasons* | *Frequency* | *Percentage* |
|---|---|---|
| Policy of the organisation | 7 | 77.8 |
| Pressure of the donor agency | 1 | 11.1 |
| Peoples' demand | 2 | 22.2 |
| Demand from the staff | 2 | 22.2 |
| Realising the value/use of PRA | 6 | 66.7 |

a binding force for following participatory approaches, even though it was the donors who introduced and trained them on PRA.

The participatory approaches in the NGOs programmes in the district were introduced with the initiative of the donor agency inter cooperation. They gave training to the leaders in their partner organisations in the period of 1990 to 1993. Later the NGOs initiated to attend trainings on PRA on their own. Subsequently, those interested in the participatory approach began to apply it in their programmes. This was precipitated by suggestion by the donor agencies. The leaders among the practice of PRA were Shreayas, WWS and RASTA. Their personnel became experts in PRA and gave training to others.

As a matter of fact stakeholder participation is an important paradigm shift that has occurred in the development arena. Nevertheless, the whole development sector has a compelling force to adapt participatory approaches. According to Clark (1996), economic policy, the provision of services and infrastructure, regulations and market mechanisms are rarely targeted toward vulnerable groups. Clearly participatory development approaches are required involving complementary actions by governments and non-governmental organisations. The third sector has increasingly adopted active participation of its stakeholders in the development process. PRA, introduced as an established strategy for participatory approaches has been found very effective by the organisation and the staff and is welcomed by the people. The FGD with the staff brought out the effectiveness of PRA in the field which have stimulated them to apply it vigorously in the field. PRA was part of the project proposal and implementation plan of certain donor agencies as well. All these have led to acceptance of PRA as an important agenda of the NGO sector.

## The Stages of the Project where PRA is being applied

PRA is generally understood as a tool used in the planning process of a project. All the NGOs in this study agree that they use PRA in the planning process of their projects. But PRA has also found manifold uses in the projects of these agencies. Two-thirds of the

**Table 6.2:** The stages at which PRA is applied

| *Stages of a project* | *Frequency* | *Percentage* |
|---|---|---|
| Planning | 9 | 100.0 |
| Implementation | 6 | 66.7 |
| Evaluation | 6 | 66.7 |
| Resource mobilization | 5 | 55.6 |
| Follow up service | 3 | 33.3 |
| Capacity building | 6 | 66.7 |
| Others | 6 | 66.7 |

organisations use PRA in the implementation, evaluation, capacity building and other components of the projects. Five of the nine organisations use PRA for resource mobilising and three use PRA for follow up of programmes as well.

Capacity building happens as an effect of PRA exercises itself. The internal and external evaluations of projects and agencies have followed PRA in monitoring and evaluation. Participatory Monitoring and Evaluation (PME) is followed in Shreyas in the monitoring and monthly assessment of the people's organisations. PRA has found new applications in the local context of the NGO and in the field. Shreyas developed new PRA tools for community assessment like farm profile and NWFDA developed Vanam Janam (forest and people) and Janam Vanam (people and forest) for assessment of relationship between forest and people. But other organisations followed the existing methods and tools of PRA only.

## PRA in the CBOs

There has been a PRA workshop conducted by the NGO in their CBO in last ten years. RASTA, Shreyas and WSSS have conducted PRA in their CBOs with the inbuilt philosophy of participation. The other NGOs have done PRA workshop related to specific projects, mainly watershed projects. While BDS conducted PRA in all potential areas before formulation of the organisation, NWFDA have done PRA for the formation of the VSS. Being the leaders of their CBO the beneficiary respondents participated in them. All the respondents have attended some type of these PRA training or workshop done either in their local area or in the NGO.

**Table 6.3:** Important topics covered in trainings—response of NGOs

| Topic | Frequency | Percentage |
|---|---|---|
| PRA concept | 8 | 88.9 |
| PRA tools | 7 | 77.8 |
| Participatory Monitoring and Evaluation | 5 | 55.6 |
| Concept/theories of participation | 5 | 55.6 |
| Equipping stakeholders to participate | 7 | 77.8 |
| Training of Trainers (ToT) on PRA | 7 | 77.8 |
| Organisation Development | 2 | 22.2 |

The above Table 6.3 explains the topics covered by the NGOs in PRA workshops. All the agencies focus on the concept of PRA in the workshops. The trainings are also meant to practice the tools of PRA and capacity building for the stakeholders to participate in the exercises. In fact the NGO do PRA workshops in the CBOs for data collection or community study or programme planning under specific projects, mainly for watershed projects in the recent period. They do it for one to three days and apply different tools after briefing the concepts of participation. While the participants get an opportunity to experiment these tools by doing them collectively with facilitators of the NGO, they do not get chance to learn PRA and its tools. Seven organisations have conducted ToT (Training of Trainers) in PRA for groups inside the agency and outside the agency. Five organisations each have conducted sessions on theories of PRA and on PME. Generally, the PRA workshops and trainings by the NGOs focus on the fundamental concepts and tool of PRA.

## Programmes where PRA has been applied in the NGOs and in CBOs

The NGOs have applied participatory approaches in their various programmes. PRA has been applied largely in the income generation programmes, in the planning of projects, agriculture development activities and women empowerment programmes. Only few NGOs have used PRA in hardware components like housing so as for the software elements of education. The response of the beneficiaries regarding the programmes of application of PRA is similar to that of the NGOs. The primary areas where

**Table 6.4:** Programmes where PRA has been applied in last ten years

| Programmes of NGO | Response of NGO | | Response of Beneficiaries | |
|---|---|---|---|---|
| | Frequency | Percent | Frequency | Percent |
| Women empowerment | 7 | 77.8 | 28 | 31.1 |
| Community study | 6 | 66.7 | 16 | 17.8 |
| Planning of projects | 7 | 77.8 | 20 | 22.2 |
| Income generating programmes | 8 | 88.9 | 23 | 25.6 |
| Housing | 2 | 22.2 | 3 | 3.3 |
| Natural Resource Management (NRM) | 5 | 55.6 | 14 | 15.6 |
| Water management | 6 | 66.7 | 11 | 12.2 |
| Health programme | 5 | 55.6 | 19 | 21.1 |
| Education | 3 | 33.3 | 13 | 14.4 |
| Agriculture | 6 | 66.7 | 36 | 40.0 |
| Watershed | 6 | 66.7 | 27 | 30.0 |
| Drinking water | 4 | 44.4 | 17 | 18.9 |
| Health Insurance | 1 | 11.1 | 2 | 2.2 |
| Others | 1 | 11.1 | 1 | 1.1 |

PRA has been applied in their areas are women empowerment, agriculture development, planning of projects, income generation projects and watershed programmes. It has been less applied in programmes like housing, health and education. The opinion of beneficiaries and the NGO may vary in this matter as the NGO speaks of all PRA that they have done in their agency, while the beneficiaries look from the programmes that they have experienced in their locality. Moreover, a single project has multiple components as in watershed project which has agriculture development, natural resource management, income generation programmes and community study in itself. Another study on application of PRA by NGOs in Tamil Nadu, India too shows that it has been widely used for women empowerment programmes (Narayanasamy and Boraian, 2004). But the other priorities of the areas of PRA application are different as the areas of operation of the NGOs are different.

The Focused Group Discussion (FGD) with the staff has added new dimensions to these findings. The four pilot organisations of RASTA, Sreyas, WSSS and WWA had applied PRA in many of the above programmes and in watershed projects. The other organisations used PRA in the watershed programmes. BDS has formed the organisation itself after a community study through PRA exercise. The NWFDA too has effectively used PRA in the formation of their CBOs. They form the VSS (Vanam Samrakshana Samithi, their CBO) after doing PRA in the area. The application of PRA in water management (in Jalanidhi project) and in the watershed project are obligatory. The agencies have applied PRA in a variety of programmes.

## People's Participation in Participatory Programmes

The programme where PRA is applied has higher people's participation compared to other programmes. They include the women empowerment programmes, planning of projects, income generation programmes, agriculture and watershed. They are the flagship programmes of the organizations. The participation of people in NRM activities are an indication of their interests in the conservation of nature. The CBOs find that agriculture as the programme with highest people's participation. As shown in this study three-fourth of the respondents *vis-à-vis* members of CBOs are involved in agriculture. The other programmes with high level of people's participation—planning of projects, income generation projects, women empowerment and watershed—are programmes the NGOs opined to have large peoples participation. The

**Table 6.5:** People's participation in various programmes

| *Programmes of NGO* | *Response of NGOs* | | *Response of Beneficiaries* | |
|---|---|---|---|---|
| | *Frequency* | *Percent* | *Frequency* | *Percent* |
| Women empowerment | 7 | 77.8 | 14 | 15.6 |
| Community study | 3 | 33.3 | 4 | 4.4 |
| Planning projects | 6 | 66.7 | 11 | 12.2 |
| Income generating programmes | 5 | 55.6 | 17 | 18.9 |
| Housing | 0 | 0.0 | 0 | 0.0 |
| Natural Resource Management (NRM) | 5 | 55.6 | 8 | 8.9 |
| Water management | 4 | 44.4 | 3 | 3.3 |
| Health programme | 3 | 33.3 | 7 | 7.8 |
| Education | 2 | 22.2 | 8 | 8.9 |
| Agriculture | 6 | 66.7 | 36 | 40.0 |
| Watershed | 6 | 66.7 | 17 | 18.9 |
| Drinking water | 1 | 11.1 | 1 | 1.1 |
| Health Insurance | 0 | 0.0 | 0 | 0 |
| Others | 1 | 11.1 | 0 | 0 |

individual beneficiary schemes like housing, education and health do not use participatory methods and have no popular participation.

The qualitative data collected from the staff, the observation from the beneficiaries and the heads of the organisation too corroborate the analysis of the above facts. PRA has undisputedly contributed to encouraging mass participation in programmes. PRA workshop in the village is an event where people from every walk of life participate. PRA has a methodology, opines the staff who facilitated the community level PRA workshops, which can attract people and give space to every individual present there. High people participation also contributes to the acceptance of the project by the people and making it a success by themselves.

*Type of People attending PRA Workshops*

Women have been the main field level stakeholders of the NGO activities so as in the PRA activities as well. Adult men and women are approximately in the age-group of 35 to 65, the young men and women are in the age-group of 18 to 35, the elderly above 65 and the children below 18. All the agencies opined that adult women participate the maximum in the PRA workshops, followed by young women (often married), adult men and young men.

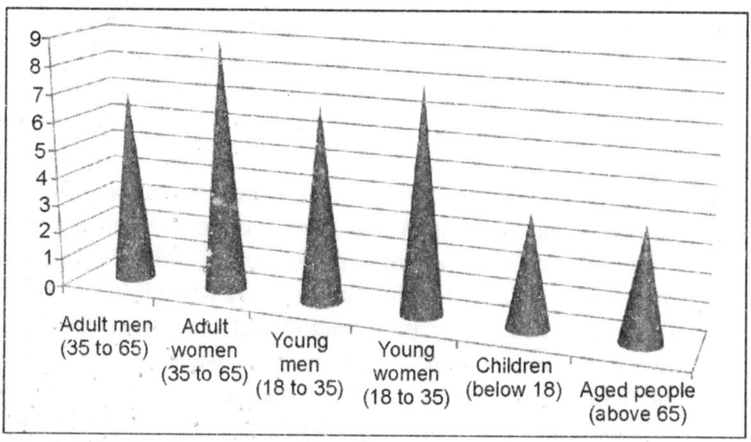


**Fig. 6.1:** Type of people participating in PRA

Children and aged participate in few numbers in the PRA workshops. The beneficiaries too opine similar to the NGO regarding the type of people participating the PRA workshops. The adult women, followed by young women, adult men and young men attend the PRA sessions. The participation of the children and aged are limited.

The staff who facilitated PRA in the field too gave a similar picture of people participation. The adult men, mainly the leaders of the CBOs take leadership in the programmes, while adult women gradually come to active involvement. The youth too join the session making it very interesting. The organisers encourage the aged in the locality for collecting data on the history of the local area. The children come to witness the whole event, though their role for active involvement is restricted.

Muraleedharan (2006) too has found profound and active participation of men and women in the Gram Sabha meetings of the local self-government in Kerala. One would be surprised to see the presence of mothers with feeding babies in the Gram Sabha meetings. The NGOs sector woos more women than men. In other parts of the world too, NGOs have implemented several projects for increasing the participation of women in civil society (Pandey, 2004). All these points to the deep social consciousness among the female population of Kerala. The nature of people's participation in PRA workshops challenges the conservative concepts of participation. People enthusiastically participate in the discussions, drawings, and in correcting, modifying and recording the data. They challenge the facilitators in certain matters and correct one another. The staff feels that the best form of people's participation is observed in PRA workshops. The participation blurs the gender, class, caste, education and religious differences of the community and gives a collective sensitivity to the community. It also challenges the notion of individual benefit for participation. Many people join the PRA workshops knowing that they may not get any individual benefit, but with the hope that the community would benefit in many ways.

The beneficiaries pointed out the reasons for why people do not participate in PRA workshops. The most important reason is that PRA was conducted at the time inconvenient for the people.

**Table 6.6:** Reasons for not participating in the PRA programmes—response of beneficiaries

| *Reasons* | *Frequency* | *Percent* |
|---|---|---|
| People are not interested in the activities of the NGOs | 23 | 25.6 |
| Programmes are conducted at the time inconvenient for the people | 38 | 42.2 |
| Do not have opportunity for all categories of people to involve in the programme | 3 | 3.3 |
| Women are restricted for participating in a programme conducted in local places | 15 | 16.7 |
| Others | 3 | 3.3 |

As discussed above the timing of PRA often coincident with the work time of most community people. One-fourth of the beneficiaries have the opinion that people are not interested in the activities of NGOs. Even though women outnumber men in public participation, there are still religious and social factors restricting women from attending public programmes like PRA. Three respondents commented that the programme is not open so that all categories of people can attend it.

Muraleedharan (2006), studying the participation of people in the Gram Sabha in Kerala identified that the major reason for non-participation is no time for the people, followed by no interest in such participatory development programmes. The issue of permission from male members at home for attending public programmes for the women too hampered their participation in the government programmes. The NGO sector too profiles similar reasons for non-participation of people. There may be multiple factors causing indifferent/lethargic to community participation by the groups and community (Mukherjee, 1997). In such situations it is important to discover ways to inspire the community or selected individuals to participate for furthering community objectives. According to Jennifer (1996), the problem with modelling participation is that participatory processes are non-linear and cyclical. The process interacts with intermediate outcomes and in turn influences the process. The important reason for participation remains to be the immediate benefit that the participants get from the programme.

***PRA Tools***

The NGOs apply various tools of PRA in practice. All the agencies have used mapping – social and resource – tools in the PRA. This has been the tool most frequently used by the NGOs. The tools of daily routine analysis, Semi Structured Interview (SSI), Focused Group Discussion (FGD) and wealth ranking have been used by eighty per cent of organisations. The other popularly used tools are venn diagram, time line, key informant interview, inflow and outflow and seasonal diagrams. Five of the nine agencies have applied the tools of participatory diagramming, pair wise ranking, SWOT analysis and problem tree. The indigenous knowledge of the community has been extracted through the folklores and case and stories by the organisations. These findings are similar to those of the tools used by the NGOs in Tamil Nadu. They too have Mapping, SSI, Focussed Group Discussion, Seasonal calendar, Ranking exercises, Venn diagram and Time line as the first seven most used tools (Naranasamy and Boraian, 2004).

**Table 6.7:** The PRA tools used by the NGOs and their frequency

| *PRA Tools* | *Response of NGOs* | | | | *Response of beneficiaries* | | | |
|---|---|---|---|---|---|---|---|---|
| | *Tools applied* | | *Frequency of application* | | *Tools applied* | | *Frequency of application* | |
| | *Fre-quency* | *Per-cent* | *Fre-quency* | *Per-cent* | *Fre-quency* | *Per-cent* | *Fre-quency* | *Per-cent* |
| Social mapping | 9 | 100 | 7 | 77.8 | 67 | 74.4 | 24 | 26.7 |
| Resource Mapping | 9 | 100 | 6 | 66.7 | 69 | 76.7 | 25 | 27.8 |
| Seasonal Calendars | 7 | 77.8 | 4 | 44.4 | 41 | 45.6 | 6 | 6.7 |
| Daily Routines Analyses | 8 | 88.9 | 5 | 55.6 | 29 | 32.2 | 9 | 10.0 |
| Semi Structured Interviews (SSI) | 8 | 88.9 | 5 | 55.6 | 10 | 11.1 | 0 | 0.0 |
| Key informant interview | 7 | 77.8 | 2 | 22.2 | 4 | 4.4 | 0 | 0.0 |
| Time line | 7 | 77.8 | 4 | 44.4 | 17 | 18.9 | 1 | 1.1 |
| Chapatti (Venn) Diagrams | 7 | 77.8 | 6 | 66.7 | 30 | 33.3 | 2 | 2.2 |
| Participatory Diagramming | 5 | 55.6 | 0 | 0.0 | 3 | 3.3 | 0 | 0.0 |
| Pair-wise ranking and scoring | 5 | 55.6 | 5 | 55.6 | 18 | 20.0 | 9 | 10.0 |
| Matrix ranking | 6 | 66.7 | 3 | 33.3 | 4 | 4.4 | 1 | 1.1 |
| Inflow outflow diagrams | 7 | 77.8 | 5 | 55.6 | 24 | 26.7 | 2 | 2.2 |
| Case and stories | 4 | 44.4 | 3 | 33.3 | 2 | 2.2 | 0 | 0.0 |
| Folk-lore, songs and poetry | 3 | 33.3 | 1 | 11.1 | 2 | 2.2 | 0 | 0.0 |
| Wealth ranking | 8 | 88.9 | 0 | 0.0 | 24 | 26.7 | 8 | 8.9 |
| Transect walk | 6 | 66.7 | 0 | 0.0 | 30 | 33.3 | 3 | 3.3 |
| Focussed Group Discussion (FGD) | 8 | 88.9 | 0 | 0.0 | 58 | 64.4 | 12 | 13.3 |
| SWOT analysis | 5 | 55.6 | 0 | 0.0 | 17 | 18.9 | 10 | 11.1 |
| Problem tree | 5 | 55.6 | 0 | 0.0 | 38 | 42.2 | 4 | 4.4 |

Even though the agencies have applied these tools, all of them are not used frequently. The most frequently used tool is social mapping, followed by resource mapping and venn diagram. Daily routine analysis, SSI, inflow and outflow and pair-wise ranking and scoring are the other tools largely applied by the organisations. Next they apply timeline and seasonal calendars followed by the matrix ranking and cases and stories. The last rank in the frequency of application goes to the key informant interview and to the use of folklores. The NGOs have answered this question in the order of the frequency of the application of the tool. The tools that received the least ranks have been hardly used by the organisations.

The beneficiaries too have responded similar to that of the NGOs regarding the PRA tools applied. The response of the beneficiaries is limited to their interaction with the tools applied in the PRA workshop conducted in their localities. (Many of the beneficiaries have attended only one workshop done in their areas, in which they came across different tools). Moreover, the beneficiaries have involved in the application of tools facilitated by the NGO personnel, and were usually not concerned and aware about the names of the tools.

Social and resource mapping stand at the top of list of tools used by the NGOs. While two-third of the beneficiary respondents commented that they were exposed to FGD in the PRA workshops, seasonal calendar have been used by 46 per cent of respondents, problem tree by 42 per cent and transect walk, venn diagram and daily routine analysis by one-third of the respondents. Inflow outflow diagram, wealth ranking, pair-wise ranking and time line have been applied in the grassroot level by the NGOs, say the beneficiary respondents.

The frequency of use of tools is similar to the ranking in the application of the tools. Social and resource mapping rank first in the frequency of the tools. Focussed Group Discussion followed by the SWOT analysis, daily routine analysis, pair-wise ranking and wealth ranking and seasonal calendars. The data on the frequency of application of the tools is limited to the exposure of the respondents, which are usually one or two PRA workshops. There are certain differences in the opinion of the NGOs and beneficiaries regarding the PRA tools applied and their frequency.

While the NGOs and staff responded from their whole experience of PRA done by their agency in the last ten years in different places, the beneficiaries responded from their limited exposure of attending one or two PRA workshops in their local areas. Moreover, the name of tools may not be familiar to them and they have replied with explanation of the tools to them. Nevertheless, the frequently used tools are similar in the response of both the agency representatives and the beneficiaries.

The qualitative data collected from the staffs of the NGOs who have facilitated the PRA exercises in the field have responded very similar to the opinions of the NGOs and the beneficiaries. The mapping exercise alone is capable of drawing lot of data about the community. Hence, they have been used the maximum and with maximum peoples participation. The other important tools used are the seasonality, time line, daily routine analysis, focussed group discussions, pair-wise ranking and *chapati* diagram. The NGOs have their choice of frequently used tools depending upon their need. For example, BDS used matrix ranking most importantly in the planning of their projects than other tools. The NWFDA devised new tools like Vanam Janam (forest and people) to do PRA and applied it in their workshops. There were differences in the frequently used tools by the GONGO and other NGOs. The use of tools depended on the nature of the project and the purpose of PRA. Mapping found high use in the watershed projects *vis-à-vis* all other projects and matrix ranking was very effective in the selection of an income generation programme.

### *Effectiveness of PRA Tools*

Table 6.8 shows the response of the NGOs and the beneficiaries on the effectiveness of the PRA tools used. The more used tools have been found more effective. It may also be due to the reverse effect that the more effective tools have been used more. The mappings followed by *chapati* diagram, seasonal calendars, ranking and scoring, daily routine analysis, inflow and outflow, time line and SSI have been found the most effective PRA tools by the NGOs. In the perception of the beneficiaries too the maps

**Table 6.8:** Effectiveness of PRA tools

| *PRA Tools* | *Response of NGOs* | | *Response of Beneficiaries* | |
|---|---|---|---|---|
| | *Frequency* | *Percent* | *Frequency* | *Percent* |
| Social mapping | 7 | 77.8 | 28 | 31.1 |
| Resource Mapping | 7 | 77.8 | 29 | 32.2 |
| Seasonal Calendars | 3 | 33.3 | 5 | 5.6 |
| Daily Routines Analyses | 5 | 55.6 | 6 | 6.7 |
| Semi structured interviews | 4 | 44.4 | 0 | 0.0 |
| Key informant interview | 3 | 33.3 | 0 | 0.0 |
| Time line | 4 | 44.4 | 1 | 1.1 |
| Chapati (or Venn) Diagrams | 5 | 55.6 | 7 | 7.8 |
| Participatory Diagramming | 0 | 0.0 | 0 | 0.0 |
| Pair-wise ranking and scoring | 5 | 55.6 | 10 | 11.1 |
| Matrix ranking | 2 | 22.2 | 0 | 0.0 |
| Inflow outflow diagrams | 5 | 55.6 | 1 | 1.1 |
| Case and stories | 1 | 11.1 | 0 | 0.0 |
| Folk-lore, songs and poetry | — | — | 0 | 0.0 |
| Wealth ranking | — | — | 1 | 1.1 |
| Transect walk | — | — | 5 | 5.6 |
| Focus group discussion | — | — | 14 | 15.6 |
| SWOT analysis | — | — | 8 | 8.9 |
| Problem tree | — | — | 3 | 3.3 |

have been found to be the effective PRA tools. Focussed Group Discussion, Pair-wise ranking, SWOT analysis, *Chapati* diagram, Daily routine analysis and Transect walk were the other effective tools in their ranking. However, the opinion of the beneficiaries is limited to the few PRA workshops they have attended. Certain tools, which the beneficiaries found useful, have not been useful by the beneficiaries; so certain tools perceived effective by the NGOs are not effective in the view of the beneficiaries. While the NGOs have applied the tools many times, the beneficiaries have been exposed to them only a few times. The mapping—social and resource—have been outstandingly the most used and most effective PRA tools. The staff too highlighted this in discussion with them. The other frequently used tools have ranked the highest in their effectiveness too.

### *Results of Participatory Programmes*

Participatory approaches implemented through PRA have brought forth quality changes in beneficiaries in their personal context

**Table 6.9**: Benefits acquired by Application of Participatory Approaches—Response of Beneficiaries

| Benefits of PRA | Frequency | Percent |
|---|---|---|
| Participation of the people increased | 52 | 57.8 |
| Got more accurate data | 44 | 48.9 |
| Transparency in the activities | 25 | 27.8 |
| Empowerment of the participants | 35 | 38.9 |
| Easy documentation | 8 | 8.9 |
| Easy interaction with the people | 40 | 44.4 |
| Clear assessment of the situation of the society | 49 | 54.4 |
| Enthusiasm of using a new methodology | 22 | 24.4 |
| Opportunity for making remarks without any restriction | 31 | 34.4 |
| More information with less time | 22 | 24.4 |
| Owning by people | 7 | 7.8 |
| Takes up leadership in community | 3 | 3.3 |
| Focus upon details of problems | 7 | 7.8 |
| Others | 2 | 2.2 |

and in their relation with the agency. PRA has been an empowering process (Mukherjee, 1993). The beneficiaries commented that the participation of people increased as a result of application of PRA. Narayansamy and Boraian (2004) found similar benefits of PRA when used by NGOs in Tamil Nadu. It has helped in getting a clear assessment of the situation of their community. The other benefits pointed out by majority of population are collection of accurate data and easy interaction with others in the community. The facilitative staff added that the community people take leadership in applying these tools, become creative and enrich themselves with new insights of their own area. The beneficiaries opined that it has helped them to make remarks without any restrictions. The use of tools of PRA has been very enthusiastic and it has contributed to the transparency of the programmes among the people. PRA has been viewed a methodology to collect more data in less time. Different from other social work practices, PRA has opened new vistas of participatory, enthusiastic, creative and unrestricted involvement of people leading to their empowerment and data collection.

The experiences of participatory approaches around the globe vouch for advantages it has brought forth in the success of development projects. The World Bank has undertaken a survey of twenty-five Bank financed projects which indicate a strong relation between project success and the participation of grassroot organisations (Clark, 1996). The World Bank has been deriving more insights from public consultations including NGOs. Such consultations are very effective where all parties are prepared to be objective and learn from each other. The application of PRA by the NGOs in Wayanad brings a global significance in this context where global leaders in development listen to small field application of local NGOs.

**Table 6.10:** Benefits of PRA for the beneficiaries—response of NGOs

| *Benefits of PRA* | *Frequency* | *Percent* |
|---|---|---|
| Creates self awareness | 6 | 66.7 |
| Takes up leadership in the community | 8 | 88.9 |
| A sense of group feeling | 7 | 77.8 |
| Joyous and happy in doing the PRA exercise | 6 | 66.7 |
| Freely express their feelings | 7 | 77.8 |
| Empowerment of deprived people | 6 | 66.7 |
| The people recognize the different dimensions of the project | 3 | 33.3 |
| Facilitates participatory decision-making | 7 | 77.8 |
| Comprehensible for common man | 3 | 33.3 |
| Interesting as it is visually appealing | 5 | 55.6 |
| Personal/family-wise change | 1 | 11.1 |

The agencies too commented that the PRA exercise has been of great benefit to the participating community. The NGOs have commented that it helped to develop leadership skills among the people capable of becoming leaders of the community and organisation. The agencies strongly felt that the PRA process helped to develop a group feeling among the community, to freely express their feelings and facilitates participatory decision-making. This process helped to create self awareness, empower the deprived groups and leaves them with the joyous experience of doing a participatory workshop. The PRA tools are visually appealing, comprehensible to all kinds of people and help to recognize the different dimensions of the project. Participation in the PRA workshop leaves a memorable experience with the people making them feel empowered for participating in their own development. According to Norton (1998), in most cases the specific purpose of policy research using participatory methods is to make available to secondary stakeholders certain kinds of information about how primary stakeholders view and analyse key issues in their lives. The insiders and outsiders benefit from the learning of PRA exercises (FAO, 1989). The primary focus of Participatory Assessment, Monitoring and Evaluation (PAME) an offshoot of PRA, is on the information needs of the communities, while the secondary focus is on the information needs of the project. The participating community is put first even in the learning objective of the PRA. The beneficiaries ratify this fact by their response that they come to know more about the project, the NGO and their own situations through PRA.

**Table 6.11:** Changes in the NGOs programmes due to PRA activities–response of beneficiaries

| *Changes* | *Frequency* | *Percent* |
|---|---|---|
| Increased the participation of the people | 48 | 53.3 |
| Increased the belief in NGOs | 26 | 28.9 |
| Got more acceptance for the activities of NGOs | 22 | 24.4 |
| Get more awareness about the programmes | 43 | 47.8 |
| People become more aware about their status | 38 | 42.2 |
| Others | 2 | 2.2 |

The agencies felt that participation of people increased as a result of applying participatory approaches to the programmes. It helped to get more awareness about the programmes of the organisation. On their end, the community became more aware of their own status—socially, economically and historically through historical time lines and other tools. The transparent process of participation increased the belief of people in the NGO and gave more acceptances for its activities. Meenai (2009) comments that participatory approaches have been able to deepen and intensify the voices of the marginalised. The important change in the application of PRA lies in facilitating the mainstreaming of the marginalised through the projects of the NGOs.

## Challenges in the Application of Participatory Approaches

### *Drawbacks of PRA*

Along with the advantages of PRA it has certain challenges as

**Table 6.12:** Drawbacks of the PRA

| *Drawbacks of PRA* | *Response of Beneficiaries* | | *Response of NGOs* | |
|---|---|---|---|---|
| | *Frequency* | *Percent* | *Frequency* | *Percent* |
| Effectiveness depends on the interest and capacity of the facilitators | 17 | 18.9 | 8 | 88.9 |
| Costlier than other methods | 18 | 20.0 | 3 | 33.3 |
| Reporting is strenuous | 5 | 5.6 | 3 | 33.3 |
| Time consuming | 21 | 23.3 | 2 | 22.2 |
| The data collected is not accurate | 3 | 3.3 | NA | NA |
| Authenticity of data challenged when presented back to the community | — | — | 4 | 44.4 |
| Others | 2 | 2.2 | NA | NA |

well. The beneficiaries found it as a time consuming process. In terms of cost too, the beneficiaries feel that it is costlier than other procedures like survey. The cost of the PRA is spent by the NGOs. The community feels that the benefits of the PRA depend largely on the capacity of the facilitators. The NGOs too feel that the major drawback of PRA is that the effectiveness of this method is largely dependable on the interest and the capacity of the facilitators. Certain beneficiaries felt that the documentation process is strenuous and data collected was not necessarily accurate. Four out of nine agencies have expressed concern over the authenticity of data collected through PRA. The reporting and cost factors too are concerns of one-third of the agencies.

The drawbacks of PRA are primarily attributed to the issue of the capacity of the facilitators. The quality of the staff doing PRA in the field was important in the success of the programme. Even though it is said to be more time consuming than other methods in the perception of the community people, PRA consumes less time compared to survey or other method in data collection. Certain agencies and people felt that the data collected through PRA may not be authentic as it is not collected in a scientific way. The staff opined that even though the authenticity of data may be challenged, PRA is not meant for scientific data. The data served the purpose it is expected to and the data collected is adequate for purpose it is meant for.

**Table 6.13:** Problems faced in field application of PRA

| *Problems* | *Response of Beneficiaries* | | *Response of NGOs* | |
|---|---|---|---|---|
| | *Frequency* | *Percent* | *Frequency* | *Percent* |
| Difficulty to get people | 37 | 41.1 | 3 | 33.3 |
| People do not participate | 31 | 34.4 | 1 | 11.1 |
| Disagreement among people | 20 | 22.2 | 5 | 55.6 |
| Inability to convene at suitable places | 14 | 15.6 | 3 | 33.3 |
| Inconvenient timings for the people | 10 | 11.1 | 5 | 55.6 |
| Domination of few people | 4 | 4.4 | 4 | 44.4 |
| People keep high expectation about it | 22 | 24.4 | 5 | 55.6 |
| Issues in managing logistics | 8 | 8.9 | 0 | 0.0 |
| Tool based problems | 1 | 1.1 | 1 | 11.1 |

One of the important problems faced in the field of the application of PRA is the difficulty to get people for the programme. The community responded that some persons are passive observers in the PRA exercises. But non-participation of the people present was a problem only for one agency. People generally have an apathy towards development initiatives which is reflected in PRA as well. The campaign mood of PRA leads to high expectation among the people. This was another problem at the field level application of PRA. There have been instances where the venue of the PRA exercise resulted in disagreement among people while applying tools like social map and historical time line. The agencies too faced the challenge of managing dominating persons in the group. The convenience of time and place for the PRA has also been a minor problem in the field according to certain beneficiaries. Five out of the nine agencies had issues with the timing of doing PRA in the community and the same per cent felt that PRA led to raising the hopes of the community. The management of logistics of PRA workshop like the writing material and food arrangements was problems experienced by a handful of beneficiaries. Mobilisation of people and finding suitable place for PRA workshop were field based problems for one-third of the agencies. One agency responded that they had problems in comprehending and communicating the PRA tools to the community. Management of logistics was not a problem in the field for the agencies. On the macro level, the multi-PRA sessions conducted by the NGOs minimize the problems faced at the field level.

The qualitative analysis added to the data on the field based issues of PRA on the perception of beneficiaries as well as of the NGOs. It is generally difficult to get people into the PRA workshops. PRA is done at least for one full day and up to three full days, on day times. This may cause loss of labour for the daily wage earners and the agriculturists. This is the reason long programmes like PRA find difficult to get people. But the facilitators agree that those who join the spirit of the PRA stay back for the consecutive days and the number of people in the following days does not get decreased. The problem of timing happens due to this risk of conducting PRA on work time of the community people.

Robert Chambers, the father of PRA, himself has mentioned the drawbacks of the PRA. Participatory methods are time consuming for local people: PRA methods, especially the visual ones like mapping, diagramming and matrices, tend to be fun and to engage peoples full attention, but sometimes for hours; and poor people time is not costless (Chambers, 1998). He also cautions about expectations are liable to be raised. After being helped to analyse their conditions, problems and opportunities, people often expect action but with facilitators in a policy research mode (and preparation of project for many NGOs) not concerned with planning of action, follow up may not be feasible. Mukherjee (1997), too cautions that the community is interested in quick and immediate results from collaborative action. However, this may not be possible for there is a time lag between making of an action plan and in implementing that plan and achieving results. Every NGO has to limit the process to the essential requirements of the exercise (optimal ignorance), be transparent and mould local ways of PRA practices without the people feeling any undue expectation.

The location of doing PRA is usually the house yard of community members or a community hall, which could be even the office of the local club or an open space. These locations are sometimes insufficient to include the whole population and for applying várious tools. But they are managed well, the facilitators argue. Even though there develops difference of opinion among people over data derived from the tools, they have never gone to conflicts beyond the managing capacity of the facilitators. The facilitators feel that when compared to the advantages of PRA these are manageable problems for the NGO and the staff.

**Table 6.14:** Difficulties faced at facilitators level—response of NGOs

| *Problems* | *Frequency* | *Percentage* |
|---|---|---|
| Inadequate knowledge | 4 | 44.4 |
| Skills in practicing PRA | 3 | 33.3 |
| Implementation without proper vision of the tools | 1 | 11.1 |
| Failing to establish rapport with people | 1 | 11.1 |
| Lack of coordination and inadequate preparation among the PRA team | 4 | 44.4 |
| Insecurity feelings of shedding power to the people | 2 | 22.2 |
| Failing to make arrangements and contact with people | 2 | 22.2 |

The competency of the facilitators is very important in PRA. The agencies comment that they face certain difficulties at this end. An important problem with the facilitators is the lack of knowledge on PRA concepts and tools. Another similar problem faced by four agencies was the lack of coordination among the field staff and lack of preparation among the PRA team. The facilitators require adequate skills in implementing PRA tools effectively, lack of which was a problem for one-third of the agencies. Very interestingly two agencies, one including the government agency felt that their staff had apprehensions about shedding power to people through PRA. Two agencies had difficulty with staff that did not make proper contacts and arrangements with the community prior to the workshop.

According to Bikshan *et al.* (1998), PRA exercises are cheaper, faster and should be in principle, be more humane than others; the conventional consultant approach is usually very expensive and disempowers local people by extracting their knowledge. But PRAs require considerable preparation and planning by professionals. The preparation for the workshop is directly proportionate to the results of the PRAs. The agencies engage experienced staff to do PRA and the juniors assist them to learn the process. The staff generally feels that they are successful in achieving the goals of the PRA workshops. The above said difficulties are faced in the process but the staff is competent to manage them well. Ultimately, the staff observe, the success of PRA lies in getting people involved in the process.

**Table 6.15:** Measures taken to overcome the PRA

| *Measures taken* | *Frequency* | *Percentage* |
|---|---|---|
| Participation at planning level | 5 | 55.6 |
| Participation at implementation level | 4 | 44.4 |
| Representative committees | 1 | 11.1 |
| Inbuilt system of participation in the organisation and projects | 2 | 22.2 |
| Representation of people's representatives | 2 | 22.2 |
| Documentation of PRA practices | 2 | 22.2 |
| Documentation division at the NGO | 3 | 33.3 |

The NGOs take measures to overcome the issues related to PRA in the field. Most of the NGOs ensure participation at the planning and implementation levels of the projects and of the organisation. One-third of the respondent organisations have their own separate division to document the proceedings of the NGO. The reports and charts prepared in the PRA workshops are kept securely in all the NGO offices. Participation is an inbuilt system for two organisations and the same number maintain people's representatives in the organisations and in projects. The efforts of the NGOs to overcome problems of PRA at the field and facilitators level find result as well.

## Participatory Approaches in Organisations

The NGOs follow participatory approaches in the management of the organisations They adapt different strategies for ensuring participation in their organisation.

**Table 6.16:** Means to ensure participatory approach in the NGOs

| *Means* | *Frequency* | *Percentage* |
|---|---|---|
| Regular meeting involving all staff | 9 | 100 |
| Workshop on policy and programme formulations | 9 | 100 |
| Established systems for feedback to authorities | 5 | 55.5 |
| Regular PME | 5 | 55.5 |

One of the best means to ensure participatory approach was regular staff meeting involving all staff. All the organisations conducted workshops on formulation of policy and programmes of the agency where the opinion of all stakeholders is taken to consideration. Five organisations had established systems of feedback from the field to the organisation that ensures the feedback' of grassroot level people to the organisations in the decision-making process. The use of PME (Participatory Monitoring and Evaluation), an offshoot of PRA, shows the advance stage of participation in the NGOs. Five organisations follow PME in their organisations. But the FGD with staff revealed that PME is regularly followed only in one organization (Shreyas).

## Difference between GONGO and NGO

The research covered eight NGOs and one Government organised NGO. The department of forests, of the State government formed Forest Development Agency at Divisional offices of the Forest Department with the purpose of coordinating the efforts of the Forest Department for forest conservation with that of the people. This was part of the policy of the Participatory Forest Management (PFM) of the national government. There exists FDAs in many parts of the State. They coordinate the grassroot level Vanam Samrakshana Samities (VSS). The VSS is formed after doing PRA in the area. The geographical area of conservation for one VSS and the strategies of conservation are formed through PRA. The PRA is repeated after certain period (five years) to rearrange the VSS. The FDA has devised certain new tools like Vanam Janam (forest and people) to assess the forest and evolve conservation efforts.

One of the NGOs (BDS) was different from other that this agency was established with specific purpose of diary promotion and have not received foreign fund. BDS did vast PRA before establishing the organisation. In fact, the data collected through PRA was very significant for the formation of the organisation as such. The tool they used and found more effective was matrix ranking than the mappings, which many other agencies found most useful. The government initiated agencies have utilised PRA with its true sense and purpose. The formation of the organisation and CBOs were done through PRA. The tools they have frequently applied were different from those used by typical NGOs. While the NGOs used PRA in implementation of their projects, the GONGOs used it for the formation of the organisation and the CBOs.

The triangulation has led to important findings in the application of participatory approaches. All the sources of information, the NGOS, the staff and the beneficiaries have found PRA as the best means for people's participation. The NGOs have applied PRA in many programmes and at various stages of the projects. The tools of social mapping, resources mapping, seasonal calendars, and matrix and venn diagrams have been used maximum by the NGOs. These tools have been found the most useful as well. The adult and young men and women take leadership in PRA workshops. PRA practices have helped the organisations as well as the beneficiaries to reap advantages of growth and effective implementation of the projects.

The participative nature and people friendly tools of PRA have attracted people to participate in it. PRA have worked as effective means for raising the downtrodden to the mainstream of the society. The NGOs find PRA as very effective tool in implementation of the project. PRA has taken the organisation and the projects to the people. PRA has worked as an empowerment tool with the poor people. Nevertheless, the system is not free of faults. The capacity of the facilitators of PRA, the convenience of the people and the long time of PRA workshops have been challenges of PRA. The NGOs follow participatory approaches in their organisational management as well. The GONGOs used PRA in formulation of the organization and CBOs the NGOs used PRA in implementation of their projects. The choice of tools for GONGOs was different for them. PRA as an institutionalised system of participation has brought new dimensions for the participation of the marginalised.

# 7

# Learning from Field

Participation has claimed much attention of the world and NGOs have spearheaded it in different ways, especially through PRA. This research analysed how did NGOs in Wayanad district used PRA in their programmes, how did people participate in it and the benefits and challenges it brought forth. This last chapter summarizes the findings of the research and attempt for pertinent learning form the field.

## Profile of the NGOs

All the organisations studied are registered societies under the Indian Societies Registrations Act. They have a general body and an executive body and function according to the bye laws of the agency with government guidelines. Six organisations operate from their own building. The other three are comparatively small and operate from rented buildings. NWFDA, being a government agency, operates from the divisional office of the forest department of the State government. All the organisations concentrate in their home district of Wayanad for programmes. The presence of some of these organisations is through certain time bound projects like the Jalanidhi and HIV/AIDS prevention projects. Three organisations have regular offices in other districts.

All the organisations have paid and voluntary staff supporting the field level activities, who are usually the leaders of CBOs. The number of staff is in proportion to the size of the organisations, i.e., the large organisations have highest number of staff. The NGOs mostly employ graduates and those with lesser educational qualifications. They receive training and guidance from the organisations. Five organisations have professionally qualified social workers (MSW) and they are appointed for specific projects and in specific positions like counsellors and project managers. Five organisations have technically qualified staff. The quality of the staff influences the functioning and professionalism of the organisations. More than half of the staffs in all the NGOs are with them for more than five years. The strength of some organisations is the staff working with them for more than ten years, some of them even from the beginning of the organisation itself. But there are frequent changes in the professionally qualified personnel; the less educated and experienced tend to stay for a longer period.

The NGOs have put women at the centre of development. The priority sectors of the NGOs are women, farmers, children and scheduled tribes. All organisations have their own women's groups. Six organisations have programmes for men. Only one organisation each has some programmes for the aged and the orphans. Wayanad has a large concentration of tribal communities and eight organisations serve them. Most of them have programmes for children and farmers. But by only five organisations have programmes focused on youth and for scheduled caste communities. Six NGOs network with Panchayati Raj Institutions (PRIs) in their programmes. The orphans and the aged are the least catered to population groups by the NGOs. The main scheme of NWFDA is forest protection and they have various social development programmes to supplement them.

The largest number of peoples groups is the SHGs for women, followed by those for men. The parent organisations form the grassroot level SHGs under federations. Seven NGOs have federations of women SHGs while four have federations for men. Eight NGOs have groups of children and five have groups for aged. The NWFDA has Vanam Samrakshana Samity (VSS), which serves the purpose of forest protection, the prime agenda of the FDA. BDS has only farmers groups formed with the aim of promotion of dairying. The organisations with a variety of programmes have different types of CBOs while the organisations formed for specific purpose have specifically targeted programmes.

All the NGOs have programmes for financial advancement of their target groups through different income generation programmes, including micro enterprises by six organisations. Most of them are involved in health care, education promotion, agriculture development, watershed, women empowerment, livestock development, sanitation, environmental conservation and legal literacy programmes. All of them have some types of community based organisation in the form of SHGs and their federations, farmers' groups, children's groups and youth clubs. The hardware components of housing, sanitary latrines and drinking water projects are implemented by half of the organisations. Eight NGOs do micro finance through CBOs while micro insurance is done by two NGOs. The NGO sector has entered into many new areas of operation with innovative strategies which use participatory approaches. The NGOs involve in a variety of activities as per the policy of the organisations and in response to the needs of the beneficiaries of the NGOs.

All the organisations depended mainly on government sponsored projects for funding. The main government aided projects are in watershed, micro enterprises, agricultural development, drinking water supply (Jalanidhi), HIV/AIDS prevention, sanitation and housing. All NGOs except government sponsored NWFDA and the BDS have received foreign aid for various projects. The NGOs mobilize funds from the Panchayati Raj Institutions, from banks and beneficiary share. The utilisation of government fund challenges the common notion of foreign funding of NGOs.

**Profile of the Beneficiaries of the NGO**

Women members participate in large numbers in the activities of the NGOs, including the PRA exercises. Women also outweigh men in the target group of the NGOs. Two-thirds of the respondents of the study were in the age group of thirty to fifty. This shows that people associated with NGOs activities are in their active age group. The majority of the participants in the NGOs activities are married. Eighty-nine per cent of respondents are married. The participation of either the husband or wife is the indication of family for involvement in NGOs activities.

The religion-wise distribution of the respondents is in proportion with the religious distribution of the district as well. The Hindus and Christians, who constitute the largest population on the district, constitute about forty-eight per cent each of respondents. The social involvement of Muslim, especially women among them, is restricted by religion. The NGOs, irrespective of their religious affinity, cater to people of all religions in serving society.

Sixty-two per cent of the respondents are from families which have four to six members. Nearly one-third of the respondents are from nuclear families with three or less members in their families. The mean family size of the respondents represents the cross-section of low income families in the district which have an average four or five members per house. Seventy-one per cent of the respondents have had only school education and half of them have only basic education, i.e., studied only up to lower primary school. This fact suggests that the educated do not usually participate in NGOs activities. The actual participation in development programmes of the non-government sector is by illiterate and less educated people.

The mean family income of the respondents reveals that the target groups of the NGOs are the economically backward communities. Fifty-four per cent of the respondents have a monthly family income of less than Rs. 2,000; thirteen per cent of respondents each fall in the income category of Rs. 2001–3000 and 3001–4000. The respondents are far behind the general stream of the society in their financial capacity and it indicates that the participants in development programmes of the non-government sector are from the financially backward classes. The family status of the respondents shows that agriculturists and farmers are an important target group of the NGOs. They comprise ninety per cent of the respondents representing the backward sections of the society. Obviously, the respondents hail from poor family situations.

The largest number of respondents, a quarter of them, has been associated with the respective NGOs for more than ten years. More than half of the respondents were involved for more than five years. The tenure of interaction indicates the duration of the entry of the NGO into their respective communities. This also reveals the capacity of the organisation in maintaining good relations with the target community. The respondents of the study were leaders in their community based organisations like SHGs (Self Help Groups), watershed committees and VSS (Vanam Samrakshana Samity). Two-third of them have been either president or secretary, which are the two powerful and responsible positions in the CBO. Some of the respondents have held more than one position for different terms. Ten respondents have not held any position in the CBOs. About seventy per cent of respondents are presently in leadership positions in the CBOs.

## Participation in CBOs

The members take the decisions of their community based organisations (CBO). The CBOs under the NGOs enjoy autonomy in their functioning. The role of the organisations is limited to giving suggestions. The people's groups are empowered to take decisions for their own growth. The internal democracy of the CBO is strong and participatory in nature.

The CBOs involve the participation of various other organisations and individuals who could contribute to the development efforts of the CBO. Apart from the members and leaders of the CBOs the staff of the sponsoring NGO, the heads of NGO, local representatives of political parties and the representatives of the local clubs too show interest in the programmes of the CBO. The participation of members of the local self-government in the activities of the CBO is limited. Certain specific projects have local committees consisting of the representatives of the PRIs and various departments of government. The representatives from the government department and outside agencies participate in local NGO activities to a lesser extent.

The programmes of the NGOs are done in association with other stakeholders. The staff of the agency invariably attends the programmes. Leaders of the people groups, officials of agriculture department, representatives of the donor agencies (including the government agencies) and the local Gram Panchayat are part of the decision-making structure of the NGOs. In certain projects like the watershed projects, the decision-making committee consists of the representatives of PRIs and various government departments.

**Participatory Approaches in NGOs**

The NGOs have adopted stakeholders' participation as a matter of policy in their institution and not because of the force of the donor agencies. They adopt PRA as they realise the potential and value of its use. The increased support from the people and staff has also helped in following participatory practices. Though PRA was introduced and trained by the donor agencies, the suggestion of donor agency is not binding for NGOs to follow participatory approaches.

All the NGOs use PRA in the planning process of the projects. Two-thirds of the organisations use PRA in the implementation, evaluation, capacity building and other component of their projects. Five of the nine organisations use PRA for resource mobilising as well. PRA was used in follow up services of programmes also. The professional evaluation of programmes and agencies has followed PRA in monitoring and evaluation. PME is followed in one NGO for the monitoring and monthly assessment of the people's organisations. PRA has found manifold dimensions of its use in the projects and in the agencies.

There have been PRA workshops conducted by the NGO in the CBOs in the last ten years. Being the leaders of the CBOs the respondents have participated in them. The main programme they attended was the PRA workshop conducted in their area by the NGO. A handful of the respondents have attended PRA training in the NGO. Three organisations have conducted PRA in their CBOs with the inbuilt philosophy of participation while others have done PRA workshop related to specific projects, mainly watershed projects and formation of VSS. Generally, the PRA workshops and trainings by the NGOs focus on the fundamental concepts and tool of PRA. Seven organisations have conducted ToT (Training of Trainers) in PRA for groups inside and outside the agency. Five organisations each have conducted sessions on theories of PRA and on PME.

The NGOs have applied participatory approaches in their multiple programmes. The primary areas where PRA has been applied are women empowerment, agriculture development, planning of projects, income generation projects and watershed programmes. Only a few NGOs have used PRA in hardware components of development like housing as also for the soft core elements of education. While four pilot organisations had applied PRA in many of their programmes, other organisations used PRA in the watershed programmes. One organisation (BDS) was formed itself after a community study through PRA exercise and another agency (NWFDA) used PRA in the formation of their CBOs.

The most frequently used tool is social mapping, followed by resource mapping and the use of venn diagrams. Daily routine analysis, SSI, inflow and outflow, pair-wise ranking and scoring are the other tools largely applied by the organisations. The NGOs apply timeline and seasonal calendars followed by matrix ranking, case studies and stories. The last rank in the frequency of application goes to the key informant interview and the use of folklores. The use of tools depended on the nature of the project and the purpose of PRA. The NGOs have their choice of frequently used tools depending upon their need. The tools which have been used more frequently have been found to be more effective. The mappings followed by the use of chapati diagram, focused group discussion, pair-wise ranking seasonal calendars, ranking and scoring, daily routine analysis, inflow and outflow, time line and SSI have been found the most effective PRA tools by the NGOs. The mapping—social and resource—have been outstandingly the most used and most effective PRA tools.

## People's Participation in Participatory Programmes

The programmes where PRA is applied have higher peoples participation compared to other programmes. PRA workshop in the village is an event where people from every walk of life participate and contribute. The highest people's participation is in agriculture. The other programmes with high level of participation are planning of projects, income generation projects, women empowerment and watershed. The individual beneficiary schemes like housing, education and health do not much apply PRA methodology and have less popular participation.

All the agencies opined that adult women participate the maximum in the PRA workshops, followed by young women (often married), adult men and young men. The age-group of young is approximately 18 to 35 and of adults from 35 to 65. The adult men; mainly the leaders of the CBOs take leadership in the programmes, while adult women gradually come to be actively involved. The PRA facilitators encourage the aged in the locality for collecting data on the history of the local area. The children come to witness the whole event, though their involvement is restricted. People enthusiastically participate in the proceedings such as in discussions, drawings, correcting and modifying the data, recording the data, challenging the facilitators and mutually correcting one another. The staff felt that the best form of people's participation was observed in PRA workshops. The participation blurs the gender, class, caste, education, religious and caste differences of the community and gives a collective sensitivity to the community.

The beneficiaries pointed out the reasons for why people do not participate in PRA workshops. The most important reason is that the timing of PRA workshop was not convenient for the people as it coincides with the work time of most community people. One-fourth of the beneficiaries have the opinion that people are not interested in the activities of NGOs. There are still religious and social factors restricting women from attending public programmes like PRA.

## Results of Participatory Programmes

The participation of people increased because of application of PRA. It has helped in getting a clear assessment of the situation of their community. It has helped in collection of accurate data and easy interaction with others in the community. The community people take leadership in application of tools, become creative and enrich themselves with new insights of their own issues. PRA has helped people to make remarks without any restrictions and contributed to transparency of the NGO programmes. PRA has helped to collect more data in less time. Different from other social work practices, PRA has opened new vistas of participatory, enthusiastic, creative and unrestricted involvement of people leading to their empowerment and data collection.

The participants enjoyed the PRA exercises and learn from them. PRA has helped to develop leadership skills among the people enabling them to become leaders of the community and organisation and to develop group feeling among the community, to freely express their feelings and facilitates participatory decision-making. This process has helped to create self awareness, empower the deprived groups and enjoy the experience of doing a participatory workshop. As the PRA tools are visually appealing, all the participants easily comprehend them. The transparent process of participation has increased the belief of people in the NGO and has enhanced the acceptance of its activities. The participation of the people has increased because of applying participatory approaches in the programmes. It has helped to get more awareness about the programmes of the organisation. The community has become more aware of their own social economic and historical status.

## Challenges in the Application of Participatory Approaches

The beneficiaries found it as a time consuming process. Another major drawback of PRA is that its effectiveness largely depended on the interest and the capacity of the facilitators. Certain respondents felt that the documentation process is strenuous and data collected were not necessarily accurate; but then PRA is not meant for scientific data.

One of the important problems faced in the field for the application of PRA is the difficulty to get people for the programme. The campaign mood of PRA leads to high expectations among the people. This was another problem at the field level application of PRA. The facilitators face the challenge of managing dominating persons in the group. Mobilisation of people and finding a suitable place for PRA workshops were field based problems for one-third of the agencies. On the macro level, the multi-PRA sessions conducted by the NGOs minimize the problems faced at the field level.

The agencies face certain difficulties like lack of knowledge of the staff doing PRA. The lack of coordination among the field staff, insufficient contacts and arrangements with the community prior to the workshop and lack of preparation among the PRA team are other problems at the field level. Two agencies, one including the government agency felt that their staff had apprehensions about delegating power to people through PRA. However, the staff is competent to manage these issues well and the success of PRA lies in making people involved in the process. The NGOs take measures to overcome the issues related to PRA in the field. They have their own separate division to document the proceedings of the NGO. The reports and charts prepared in the PRA workshops are kept securely in their offices. The efforts of the NGOs to overcome problems of PRA at the field and facilitators level gradually decrease such issues.

## Participatory Approaches in Organisations

The NGOs follow participatory approaches in the management of the organisations. One of the means to ensure participatory approach was to have regular staff meeting involving all staff. All the organisations conducted workshops with stakeholders for the formulation of policy. Five organisations had established systems of feedback from the field to the organisation to ensure feedback of grassroot level people to the organisation's decision-making process. Five organisations follow PME in their organisations for regular monitoring of the programme at the agency level.

The research covered eight NGOs and one Government Organised NGO (GONGO). The one GONGO (NWFDA) and the other NGO (BDS), which have not received foreign aid, formed their CBOs after doing PRA. NWFDA devised new PRA tools like Vanam Janam (Forest and People) and Janam Vanam (People and Forest) to assess the specific needs of locals in relation to the forests. The BDS was formed after doing an extensive PRA. The tools they have frequently applied were different from the typical NGOs. The government initiated agencies have utilised PRA in its true sense and purpose.

## Combating Challenges Ahead

The analysis and the findings of the research throw light on the profile of NGOs and their beneficiaries and on the application of PRA by the NGOs. There are various areas where the NGOs need to critically reflect upon their rationale of existence and nature of functioning. Along with the benefits accrued from the use of participatory approaches, there are certain gaps to be filled by its practitioners. The researcher discusses certain of those concerns and proposes suggestions.

## How will NGOs Move to Next Generation?

The study reveals that the fields of activities of NGOs continue to be conventional and repetitive. They are reactive to the needs of society rather than being proactive to social development and are not adequately updated with advanced technologies. The NGOs need to realise the changes in society and develop to meet the requirements of society and to device novel strategies for addressing them. The philosophical basis of the activities seems to be charity. There is a clarion call for a shift to a more professional approach in NGO governance. The quality and continuity of the staff are important to effectively carry out the programmes of the organisation. The agencies lack sufficiently trained and capable professional staff to manage their affairs. This has affected the application of PRA practices as well. The NGOs recruit staff from the field level volunteers and appoint them in different position once they get experience and training. While such staff stays with the organisations for a longer time the professionals do not do so. The NGOs need to recruit sufficient professionals in their organisations for more qualitative professional services.

The study shows that the sources of funds for the NGOs is depleting due to withdrawal of donor agencies from the State. The main source of funds has become the central and State governments. The NGOs need to focus on mobilisation of resources from local sources and from corporate houses. The NGOs in Kerala have not made effective attempts in this end. The documentation of the NGO activities within the organisation is inadequate. The organisation did not have accurate record of the details like date and venue of PRA done. The only reference was the statutory reports they had submitted to donor agencies and the charts used in PRA workshops. The good deeds of the NGOs are not recorded and communicated to the world outside. The NGOs need to advance their documentation skills, prolifically use technology for documentation, keep the documents well and disseminate them for others to learn.

NGOs have taken up a role of implementing the projects financed by the government or other bilateral agencies. The contribution of the NGOs to policy formulation, social legislation, knowledge creation and building theories are significant in the contemporary era. They need to resort to more research and advocacy to move in these directions and to fulfil their stated vision.

The important target groups of NGOs are women, men and farmers. The orphans, scheduled castes and the elderly are less considered while the youth and children occupy still a better position. The NGOs need to reorient themselves so as to cater the needy and invest in the youth and children which includes the presently excluded.

## Revitalising Participatory Approaches

The study reveals that the NGOs have maximum participation of people through PRA. PRA has been done as part of the specific projects and by the suggestions of donors. The NGOs could integrate participatory practices into their organizational life. They could use PRA in its multiple dimensions to ensure participation of people in all their programmes. PRA exercises have contributed to transparency and acceptance of the NGO activities and projects. Hence, the NGOs could utilise PRA in all their projects to ascertain its transparency and more acceptance by the stakeholders.

The NGOs have utilised the stereotypical tools and methodologies of participatory exercises, although two organizations attempted for innovations. The NGOs need to learn from their field experiences and device innovative ways to enhance participatory approaches. The competency, skill and knowledge base of the field level facilitators of PRA is very important for the success of the PRA exercise. The finding of the study shows that the NGOs face challenges in this context. They need to guarantee these qualities by ensuring adequate training and experience for the field level facilitators of PRA.

PRA has abundant scope for doing research work in social development. The response of the NGOs shows that PRA has not been used for research. The NGOs can use PRA for research purposes to further effectively implement their programmes. The study has found that the NGOs were not keen on the application of participatory approaches in organisational management. The participatory methods like PME could be used effectively in the management of organisations.

The initial application of PRA was largely a result of the suggestions of donor agencies and on the stipulated guidelines of the government aided development projects. The organisations have realised the value of it in enhancing the participation of stakeholders. Nevertheless, the NGOs have yet to internalise the spirit of participation and situational use of PRA as a methodology. The NGOs have done one or two PRA workshops in the field as part of the project in many locations. The community people who attended it have been exposed to these workshops only. But, the NGOs perceive the PRA from the angle of all the PRA that they have done for various projects in different locations. The NGOs have to view the application of participatory approaches from the perspective of the community people who have been exposed to only one PRA workshop.

**Further to Explore**

The researcher has not studied the reasons for the gradual changes in the application of PRA over a period of time. Such a study could reveal the changes in the acceptance and use of PRA by NGOs. This study can track the changes the PRA has undergone in the hands of NGO. Further research could explore the knowledge level of beneficiaries on PRA. The actual clarification of the beneficiary on their conceptual clarity of PRA could disclose community people's awareness on PRA. The NGOs have devised new tools and enhanced some of the existing tools of PRA according to situations. Further research can look at the innovations done at the tools of PRA by the NGOs.

The research has covered the staff, the heads of the NGOs and the beneficiaries of the NGOs in this study. Another research can study the attitudes and opinion of the donors, the locally networked organisations like local self-governments and government departments like agriculture and other organisations on PRA application by the NGOs. The long-term impact of the PRA at the agencies and at the beneficiary level is yet another area of study. Such a research can shed light on the sustainable characteristics of the participatory approaches. It may seem surprising that why NGOs did not integrate use of participatory approaches even while experiencing the magic it brings in stakeholder participation. A research can reveal why NGOs have shunned assimilating the spirit of participatory approaches in their organisations.

## Conclusion

NGOs have become a significant agent of social change in contemporary society and this book was an attempt to reveal the profile of them as well as their beneficiaries. It showed participatory approaches of NGOs in their development activities through the research. The researcher studied variables from the viewpoints of beneficiaries, NGOs and field level facilitators of the agencies. The study has substantially revealed the advantages of participatory approaches in ensuring participation of people, transparency of the project and owning up of the projects by people through PRA. PRA was the most enjoyable and participatory field level programme of the NGOs' activities for the staff and the community people. Adult women and men actively participate in the PRA programmes. The NGOs apply PRA in many fields. The facilitators use a variety of PRA tools in their participatory approaches. Nevertheless, it has certain drawbacks and challenges as well.

The research unfolded the profile of the NGOs and its beneficiaries. The NGOs in Wayanad bear the characteristics of any other voluntary agency in the State and in the nation. They operate in similar fields. Some organisations established for specific purpose—like NWFDA for forest conservation — restrict their activities to their specific areas. All the organisations have community based organisations especially of women, for men, children, farmers and aged. The profile of the beneficiaries of the NGOs depicts that they belong to the most disadvantaged sections of the people. The beneficiaries are less educated and financially backward. Married women constitute the majority of the beneficiaries of the NGOs, followed by adult men and youth. The beneficiaries cherish their long time relationship with the NGOs.

There has been a significant change in the participation of people by adapting to participatory practices and application of PRA in the programmes of the NGOs. The development projects need to identify themselves with advanced version of participatory approaches and integrate participation to every development programme and in organisation management. The study puts forward certain suggestions to improve the application of participatory practices by the NGOs in their management. The findings of the study would be useful for the academic community and practitioners on matters relating to voluntary sector and in issues relating to peoples participation. The author hopes this research would contribute to better understating of the NGOs, their beneficiaries and participatory approaches and the learning would be used in social development initiatives.

# Bibliography


Adriance, D., (1995), *PRA in a Health Education, Water and Sanitation Project in Kenya*, PLA Notes, IIED London, 22,

Anna, K.; Vandever W.; Lee, Woo.; and Anna, Maria. (1995), *The Participation of NGO in Poverty Alleviation: A Case Study of Honduras Social Investment Fund Project*, World Bank, Discussion papers, 295, 9

Arora, (1993), as quoted in Mishra, R.B.; Sing, Chandrapal., (Edts), *Struggle for Rural Development*, New Delhi, Commonwealth Publishers,

Arora, R.K., and Ahmed, A., (1990), The dynamics of development from participatory to people centred approach, in *Development Administration*, Pinto, R.; Srinivasa R. (eds). New Delhi, Himalaya.

Beveridge, Lord., and A.F. Wells., (eds.), (1949), Notes on the Future of Voluntary Social Work, in *The Evidence for Voluntary Action*, London: Allen & Unwin.

Bhattacharya, A., (2001), *Community Participation and Sustainable Forest Development: Global Perspective*, New Delhi, Concept.

Bhose, S.G.R., (2003), *NGOs and Rural Development Theory and Practice*, New Delhi, Concept Publishing Company.

Bikshan, G.; Micheal, D. and Meera, S. (1998), Village Voices Challenging Wetland Management Policies – PRA experiences from Pakistan and India in Jeremy Holland with James Blackburn, *Whose Voice? Participatory Research and Policy Change,* London, Intermediate Technology Publications.

Bob, Sam., (2008), *Participation of the Poor in Rural Development Programmes—Selected Case Studies*, New Delhi, Discovery Publishing House.

Burgress, R.G., (1984), *In the Field: An Introduction to Field Research*. London: Routledge.

Chambers, R., (1997), *Whsoe Reality Counts? Putting the Last First*, London, Intermediate Technology Publications.

Chambers, R., (1998), in Foreword of Jeremy Holland with James Blackburn, *Whose Voice? Participatory Research and Policy Change,* London, Intermediate Technology Publications.

Chandra, S., (2001), *Non-Governmental Organisations—Structure, Relevance and Functions,* New Delhi, Kanishka Publishers & Distributors.

Clark, John, D. (1996), The State, Popular Participation and the Voluntary Sector, in Jennifer, R. McCracker, (Ed.) *Participation in Practice the Experience of World Bank and Other Stakeholders*, The World Bank.

Creswell, John, W., (2003), *Research Design, Quantitative, Qualitative and Mixed Methods Approach*, New Delhi, Sage.

Dantwala, M.L., (1998), Promises to Keep, in *Social Change through Social Action*, New Delhi, Sage.

FAO (1994), *Tree and Land Tenure—Rapid Rural Appraisal Tools*, Community Forestry Filed Manual, 4, 8.

FAO (1989), *Community Forestry, Participatory Assessment, Monitoring and Evaluation*, Community Forestry Note 2, 5.

Foss, Nina and Aune, Liv., (2000, June), *PLA as a Tool in Participant Process—Orientated Evaluation in the Field of Drug Prevention Psychiatry in Norway*, PLA Notes, 38.

Gant, Kate, (2000, June), *Consultation or Active Participation? Community Arts and Participatory Appraisal Workers Working Together to Really Involve Local People in Decision-Making*, PLA Notes, 38.

Gosselink, P., and Hoeberichts, A., (1996, June), *PRA in International Agricultural Research: First Experiences in IIMI-Pakistan*, PLA Notes, 26.

Greene, J.C.; Caracelli, V.J.; and Graham, W.F., (1989), Toward a conceptual framework for mixed-method evaluation designs, *Educational and Policy Analysis*, 11(3).

Gupta, R.K., (2006), *NGOs and Development*, New Delhi, Mahaveer & Sons.

Harper, G., (2000 June), Articulating the rural voice—a case study from Northern Ireland, PLA Notes, 38.

Henn, M., *et al.*, (2006), *A Short Introduction to Social Research*, New Delhi, Vistaar Publications.

Jennifer, R. (1996), The Contribution of Peoples Participation in Jennifer, R. McCracker, (Edtd) *Participation in Practice the Experience of World Bank and Other Stakeholders*, The World Bank, 13

Joseph, M.J., (2000), Kerala Research Programme Local Level Development, Thiruvananthapuram, Centre for Development Studies, Discussion Papers, 47.

Joshi, Uma., (2001), *Understanding Communication*, New Delhi, Dominant Publishers.

Kashyap, G.B., and Gars, J.P., (Edts), (2008), *Panchayati Raj and Local*

*Governance in Rural India Vision and Mission,* Vol. XIV, New Delhi, Vistara.

Kasivelu, S.; Howes, R.; and Devavaram, J., (1995, February), *The Use of PRA in Rehabilitating Minor Irrigation Tanks*, PLA Notes, 22.

Korten, D., as quoted in Chandra, S., (2001), *Non-Governmental Organisations—Structure, Relevance and Functions,* New Delhi, Kanishka Publishers & Distributors.

Kumar, S., (Edt), (1996), *South-South Workshop on PRA: Attitudes and Behaviour*, Bangalore, Action Aid.

Lindberg, M., and Brayant, C., (2001), *Going Global, Transforming Relief and Development NGOs*, 1294 Blue Hills Avenue, Bloomfield CT 06002, USA, Kumarian Press.

Marshall, F., (1996), Can we define Voluntary Sector, in Bills, D.; Harris, M. (Edts), *Voluntary Agencies*, London, MacMillan

Meenai, Z., (2008), *Participatory Community Work,* New Delhi, Concept Publishing Co.

Mohanan, B., (2005), *Decentralized Governance and Participatory Development—Issues and Prospects*, New Delhi, Concept Publishing Co.

Mukherjee, N., (1993), *Participatory Rural Appraisal Methodology and Applications*, New Delhi, Concept Publishing Co.

Mukherjee, N., (1997), Participatory Appraisal of Natural Resources, New Delhi, Concept Publishing Co.

Mukherjee, N., (2002), *Participatory Learning and Action*, New Delhi, Concept Publishing Co.

Mukherjee, A., (2004), *Participatory Rural Appraisal, Methods and Applications in Rural Planning*, New Delhi, Concept Publishing Co.

Muraleedharan, K., (2006), *Participatory Development Issues and Lessons,* New Delhi, Serial Publications.

Narayansamy, N., and Boraian, M.P., (2005), *Participatory Rural Appraisal: The Experience of NGOs in South India*, New Delhi, Concept Publishing Company.

Norton, A., (1998), Whose Voice? Reflections from the IDS Workshop, in Jeremy Holland with James Blackburn, *Whose Voice? Participatory Research and Policy Change,* London, Intermediate Technology Publications.

Pandey, Pradeep K., (2004), Women's empowerment through their participation in the decision-making process: A comparative study on the local Government of Bangladesh and India in Stanley, Selwyn *Social Problems in Indian Perspectives for Intervention*, New Delhi, Allied.

Pearce, J., (2000), Development, NGOs and Civil Society – The Debates and its Future, in Pearce, Jenny (introduced by), *Development, NGOs and Civil Society*, Oxford, Oxfam GB.

Pocknell, S., and Annaly, D., (1995, February), *The Use of RRA in Conservation Expeditions: Experiences from Sierra Leone*, PLA Notes, 22.

Praxis, (1998), *PRA Methods Pack,* New Delhi, Praxis Institute for Participatory Practices.

Pretty, J.N., (1995 August), *Participatory Learning for Sustainable Agriculture*, World Development, Vol. 23, No. 8.

Raja, E., and Mahiba, M., (2000, December), Participatory Micrό Enterprises, *Kurukshetra*, Ministry of Rural Development, GoI, 16.

Rana, K., (2001), *Peoples Participation and Voluntary Action – Dimensions, Roles and Strategies*, New Delhi, Kanishka Publishers.

Ramesh, B., (2000), Kerala Research Programme Local Level Development, Thiruvananthapuram, Centre for Development Studies, Discussion Papers 17.

Ravindran Nair, G., (1997 October), *Social Activism in Women's Development*, Social Welfare, Ministry of Social Justice and Empowerment, GoI, 11.

Rindell, Roger C., and Robinsons, M., (1995), *Non-Governmental Organisations and Rural Poverty Alleviation*, New York, Oxford University Press.

Rodríguez, I., (1998, Oct.), *Using PRA for Conflict Resolution in National Parks: Lessons from a Venezuelan Experience in Canaima National Park*, PLA Notes.

Santhanam, M.L., (1993), Community Participation for Sustainable Development, *Indian Journal of Public Administration*, Vol. XXXIX. No. 3.

Saxena, N.C., (1998), What is meant by People's Participation?, *Indian Journal of Rural Development*, Vol. 17(1), Hyderabad.

Sharma, B.B., (Edt), (1992), *Encyclopedic Dictionary of Sociology*, Vol. 3, New Delhi, Anmol.

Sing, M., and Lal, M., (2005), Participatory Management of Natural Resources, in Mishra, G.P. and Bajpai, B.K., *Community Participation in Natural Resource Management*, Jaipur, Rawat.

Smith, C., and Freedman, A., (1972), *Voluntary Associations*, Cambridge, MA.

Srikumar, C., (2000), *Kerala Research Programme Local Level Development*, Thiruvananthapuram, Centre for Development Studies,, Discussion Papers.

Uphooff, N.T., and Cohen, J., (2003), Feasibility and Application of Rural Development Participation, in Bhose, Joel, S.G.R., *NGOs and Rural Development Theory and Practice*, New Delhi, Concept Publishing Company

Vaidyanathan, A., (2001), *Watershed Development: Reflection on Recent*

*Developments*, Kerala Research Programme Local Level Development, Thiruvananthapuram, Centre for Development Studies, Discussion Papers 43.

Vijayanad, S.M., (1996), *People's Participation in Poverty Reduction Programmes—A Study of the Integrated Tribal Development Project (ITDP) Attappady Kerala*, (unpublished) M.Phil. Thesis, New Delhi, JNU.

WCARRD, (1979), as quoted in Mohan, B. (2005), *Decentralized Governance and Participatory Development – Issues and Prospects*, New Delhi, Concept Publishing Co.

# Index